Loretta and Me

Edward J Funk

Copyright © 2015 Edward Joseph Funk. Registration # TXu 1-961-563 All rights reserved. Including the right to reproduce this book or portions thereof, in any form. No part of this text may be reproduced in any form without the express written permission of the author
ISBN: 0-9971054-4-5
ISBN-13: 978-0-9971054-4-5

All Photos from the Salvador Iglesias Collection

Permission to use from the Loretta Young estate

Chapter One: Me 5

Chapter Two: The Gauntlet: Getting by Loretta's Agent 12

Chapter Three: Meeting Loretta 21

Chapter Four: Loretta's Formidable Charm 25

Chapter Five: Meeting Loretta's Family and Friends 34

Chapter Six: Mixing with the Really Rich and Famous 45

Chapter Seven: Loretta Breaks her Silence on Gable 57

Chapter Eight: Loretta Wows Them at the Waldorf 78

Chapter Nine: The Why of Loretta's Marriage to Jean Louis 100

Chapter Ten: Estrangement with Daughter Judy 110

Chapter Eleven: Judy's Bruising Tell-all Book 120

Chapter Twelve: Flying in Loretta's Palm Springs Orbit 130

Chapter Thirteen: More Rich and Famous 142

Chapter Fourteen: The Psychic Maid 154

Chapter Fifteen: Loretta's Surprise Gift 162

Chapter Sixteen: A Movie Star's Farewell 166

Acknowledgment: for *Loretta and Me* 172

About the Author 173

Chapter One: Me

This book is about the relationship between Loretta Young and me that grew from our first meeting in December, 1989, until the day she died in August, 2000. That interview had been arranged by her agent to explore the possibility of our collaboration on her autobiography.

More than that, this book details who Loretta Young was in the last decade of her life, her family and friends, and the nature of those relationships. In those years, Loretta lived in Beverly Hills, then in both Beverly Hills and Palm Springs, and finally, in Palm Springs only. I knew those homes well, having my own key to the Beverly Hills home and was her most frequent house guest in Palm Springs. Loretta married for the third and final time in 1993 to Jean Louis, famous Hollywood courtier. I understood the reason for that marriage as well as why it succeeded.

Her daughter Judy wrote a *Mommy Dearest* type book in 1984 titled "Uncommon Knowledge." I'm the one who brought that book to Loretta; she needed to know what was in it. I'm also the one to whom she confided that Judy's writing of the book, not the book itself, presented the most painful episode in her life. It was during this period that she told me that I was her best friend. She had a couple of wonderful, lifetime friends, one being Josie Wayne, John Wayne's first wife, but she never discussed with Josie the extremely personal issues that she did with me. I know because both Loretta and Josie, during separate conversations, told me so.

How did I come into the picture? Here is where the reader would expect an introduction to my qualifications as an established writer. It will become clear in the next few pages that I had precious little experience as a writer. I did have experience of talking my way into opportunities, this being the example extraordinaire.

The next few pages will give you a thumbnail sketch of my pre-Loretta life. I wasn't particularly fascinating and that's really the point. I was just an "anybody" walking into a "somebody's" world. But the things I noticed, the things that seemed important to me, were as much influenced by who I was as who Loretta was.

I was age forty-four when I met Loretta, thirty-two years younger than she. I grew up on a farm in Indiana, an experimental farm where hybrid seed for corn was developed. Edw. J. Funk & Sons was a family-owned business and, during my growing up years, my father served as President. I went to a Catholic grade school with 10 in our eighth grade graduating class. From there I went to St. Bede Academy, a boarding school in North Central Illinois and then to Marquette University in Milwaukee, Wisconsin. I was clueless regarding a career as my Marquette years were ending, and my dad advised me to study law as he had. I was drafted out of the Indiana University Law School first year class in the spring of 1968 and was in Vietnam by Easter, 1969.

I was the fourth of six children; my distinction being that I was the only one sent to a psychiatrist at age six. My bent in life was apparently to disrupt the world as I knew it.

I managed to do well academically but was often in trouble. During grade school, I would be off the school bus by 4:15 p.m., complete my only chore of emptying the trash in time to plant myself in front of the TV for "The Early Show" at 4:30, the broadcasting of old movies by the CBS affiliate out of Chicago. I think my mom allowed this schedule because it was a distraction that would last until dinner time, buying temporary peace.

I probably first knew about homosexuals during my high school years, but I didn't see myself as one. I should have figured it out during my college years, but coming out of my Catholic, rural background, I was firmly in denial. That continued through my thirteen-and-a-half months in Vietnam and also through my mid-twenties. Coinciding with this denial was a sense of being lost and an increasing abuse of alcohol.

I worked with my older brother Jim in the future's brokerage business, and when I told him I wanted to move on, he was happy to encourage me. In my early thirties I was writing speeches and letters for my cousin Dick, my best friend, who was now the marketing director for the seed business, which by this time was out of my immediate family's control. I was also leading a secret gay life that was unsatisfactory because the "next morning" always came with a hangover, a bad hangover that could last days. Finally, I hit bottom and stopped drinking. I was age thirty-two.

Before I stopped drinking, a friend of a friend connected me to a man who was interviewing for an advertising manager for Sea World of Florida. Astoundingly, I made the cut to the final two but the opportunity went to the other guy. Now that I had stopped drinking, I was hired full time as a communications manager for the family business. It was during this period that I helped my Uncle Bill write a book about my grandfather's family and their pioneering efforts in the hybrid seed industry.

Sea World contacted me six months later, asking if I'd be interested in a position in their Ohio park, a Sea World now long gone. Eight months after that, the man who had been hired over me at the Florida park was moving up in the organization, and I was offered the position of advertising manager in Orlando.

It was only a few years later when the *Queen Mary* in Long Beach, California, offered me the position of director of marketing services. The idea of living in Southern California seemed exciting and I accepted. I had always loved movies, and as the years went on I became more and more entranced with the movies of the '30s and '40s. I think I wanted to go to California, at least in the back of my mind, because I thought there might be some way of making a living in connection with those old films, without having the least idea of what that connection might be.

Two years later, I lost my position with the *Queen Mary* when the new President wanted to incorporate what I did into what he did. He was fired three weeks later, and I was called and asked if

I wanted to return. I didn't. I was then offered a job from a local Coca Cola bottling company to manage their promotions. I turned it down. At this point, I wanted a position with less management responsibilities and more creative opportunities.

My cousin Don, now President of the seed business, came to my rescue. The company was offering incentive travel trips to their customers, and he asked me to develop marketing material for that effort. It was a major part of their marketing; the first year I worked on this endeavor, they transported 3,000 people over a six-week period to Germany. I not only previewed the destination but spent the entire six weeks in Munich with the customers. Don paid me well, and I could afford to try my hand at freelance writing when I wasn't working for him. I kept my apartment in the Belmont Shore section of Long Beach and spent more time in California than in Indiana.

I was in my mid-thirties by now and had accepted the reality that I was homosexual without actually accepting homosexuality as a respectable lifestyle. My resistance ebbed away over the years, and at age forty-two, I began dating a man fourteen years younger named Joey. It was my first homosexual relationship but I didn't' envision it would have staying power. I just didn't think that that was in the cards for gay men. I enjoyed Joey and his somewhat irreverent attitude about life. I was so buttoned up in comparison. I would go back and forth to Indiana and wherever in the world Don's incentive trips would lead me. I had done so for three years before Joey and continued for the next two. Finally, when I returned to Long Beach in September, 1988, Joey made it indisputably clear that we were washed up as a couple. I was gone too much of the time, and I had never really made a commitment to him.

I was devastated. I felt very guilty because Joey was right; I had never been willing to give him what he had been willing to give me. I had invited him into my life just enough so that I wasn't lonely but gave little back. In just a few days I began to unravel. I had started smoking marijuana after I quit drinking and became addicted to it, so much so that I couldn't go to sleep without it. Now that wasn't working and I entered a manic state in which I was only sleeping a few hours a week. I had had sleep problems all my life but this propelled the insomnia to a whole new level. I went back to Indiana to be with friends and family, but the mania was soon joined by depression and this combination culminated in a hospitalization at Billings Hospital, the University of Chicago. I was diagnosed as Bipolar II, but after several unsuccessful attempts of medication, they told me that I was too chemically sensitive for pharmacological help, and I'd have to lead my life as stress free as possible. I cynically thought to myself, "Good luck with this."

I never smoked marijuana again. It may have helped me sleep during the preceding thirteen years but my freelance writing output amounted to very little and the marijuana had been a factor. I wrote two plays which have never been produced and two episodes for a syndicated television show, THE JUDGE. I sent various letters to agents of celebrities, pitching myself as a collaborator for a biography, but seldom received a reply. When I did, the answer was no.

It took five months from the time I left Long Beach to the time I pulled myself together and returned. Then it would only take a week before my path first crossed Loretta's.

Chapter Two: The Gauntlet: Getting by Loretta's Agent

Joey met my plane when I returned to Los Angeles (We never became a couple again, but, in time, good friends). It was a Sunday evening and he brought the Calendar section of that day's *The Los Angeles Times*. It carried a notice about Loretta Young making a rare public appearance a week hence. There was a beautiful picture from her movie glory days, photographed by Horst; a classic profile of Loretta wearing a black dress with slim straps and an enormous black hat. The copy announced a fund raiser at the Los Angeles Museum of Art, Bing Theater. Two of her television shows would be shown followed by an hour of question and answer. The proceeds would go to the Museum of Radio and Television in New York. Joey knew that Loretta Young had been a favorite of mine and thought I might be interested.

I was still pretty shaky, still dealing with symptoms of depression, including the inability to concentrate. By midweek, I decided to pass on the Loretta Young event as I was wary about driving the freeways. However, when early Sunday evening rolled around, I was feeling better and I convinced myself that Sunday traffic would be light so why not give it a try?

I arrived at the Bing Theater a half hour early and went to the ticket counter only to discover that the event was sold out. As I walked away another man approached the counter, and a few seconds later I heard the ticket guy yelling at me. "Hey buddy, you're in luck. This guy's turning a ticket in." I quickly paid for it and he explained that it was open seating, first come first served. Just as I had ticket in hand, the doors opened and I scooted around bunches of people visiting with each other and managed to land a seat in the front row.

Loretta Young had had an imposing film career that began in the silent era. She turned fifteen playing Lon Cheney's leading lady in LAUGH, CLOWN, LAUGH and by the time she won 1947's Best Actress Oscar for THE FARMER'S DAUGHTER, she had been the star or leading lady in eighty films. Her leading men included greats such as Clark Gable, Cary Grant, Tyrone Power, Spencer Tracy, James Cagney and Orson Welles. But many people today remember her best for THE LORETTA YOUNG SHOW a NBC Sunday night TV staple that ran for eight years from 1953 through 1961, and then another decade in reruns. In 1957, America still loved Lucy, but a *TV Guide* poll named Loretta Young as "the most important woman in television."

Her television show was an anthology series, a format that had been popular on radio. There were no running characters; each show was different: comedy one week, suspense the next, drama the one after that. What made it THE LORETTA YOUNG SHOW was that Loretta hosted each week, introducing the shows and coming back at the end to tie everything together. She also starred in most episodes. In most people's minds who remember, what really made it THE LORETTA YOUNG SHOW was her entrance: how she opened the door, swept through it, turned to close the door so that the viewers could see both the front and back of her exquisite gown, then walked to a desk before greeting the viewers. For decades after, to say that someone "walked through a door like Loretta Young" became part of the American lexicon, conjuring up an image of commanding elegance and grace.

The seven hundred seat theater filled quickly and as the lights went down, two chairs became evident at front center stage. The host from the Museum of Radio and Television appeared. He introduced Loretta who then glided onto the stage to take her chair. Wow! At age seventy-six, her body trim and her face practically wrinkle-free, Loretta was still elegantly beautiful. She reminded me of a character in an epic movie where the heroine ages in the course of the story, only she really doesn't except for a few lines drawn here and there. She wore a fitted cream-colored suit with a matching turban. The turban seemed to say, "I'm still a star," and the applauding crowd, rising to their feet, offered their affirmation.

Loretta smiled, said hello and how happy she was to be there, and then we quickly got down to the business of watching the two episodes from her television show. She didn't always play glamorous characters in her anthology series, but she had chosen two selections in which she had. In one she played a model being stalked, and in the other she was reunited with a long lost love.

It was during the ensuing question/answer period that I realized this woman was much more intelligent, much more sophisticated, than my impressions formed from her television years. Within a year or two prior, I had read a biography of her and now felt that the authors had also missed the mark. Apparently, they had never met her.

When I drove from Long Beach that evening, I had not entertained any idea of writing a book with Loretta Young. But, as I sat there, I was convinced I could do a much better job than the one I had recently read. The experience of helping Uncle Bill with his book emboldened me. So what if one book was about a family selling seed corn and the other about a movie star? When it came down to it, telling a story in an engaging fashion was what really mattered.

There was a man sitting next to me at the theater, about my age, who told me that he had been on a cruise when Loretta had also been a passenger. I was only half listening until he mentioned he knew that she lived on Ambassador Avenue in Beverly Hills. That turned out to be handy information.

The next day I composed a letter pitching myself as a collaborator for Loretta's autobiography. Then I called the library at the Motion Pictures Arts and Sciences and said that I was a writer doing an article on Loretta Young and did she still live on Ambassador Avenue? After holding a minute I got a reply, "Yes, she lives at 1705 Ambassador Avenue" Now, I had her address.

Here is the letter I sent:

March 24, 1989
Dear Miss Young:

I was in last night's audience at the Bing Theater and thoroughly enjoyed the evening. What an excellent actress and lovely lady you are! I had a question for you last night but did not have the opportunity to ask it. My question was, "Miss Young, you tell such wonderful anecdotes. Why don't you tell your autobiography from the prospective of your life that you have now?"

Here's my pitch on why you should write your story. The largest book reading market today is the baby boom generation. We range from early-thirties to mid-forties. As children, television impacted us differently than it has following generations. We were allowed an innocence that made possible a very personal relationship with a star like you. Because of the tone of your stories, we connected with you in a very moral way.

What's so fascinating about you is that you're both so moral and profane. Last night you mentioned God and a minute later you said that you wished that you had been on television fifteen years later so that you could have raked in the big bucks. I loved it. You were fun, so much more than I would have imagined. Your book would be fun, too.

You also said that you don't believe in luck, but that you believe that wonderful things come your way if you approach life with a caring attitude. Open your mind to the good you could do by writing your story.

You mentioned that it's your policy to work with professionals. So, why would you bother with me? No one else can do what I can do for you. I am who I am from forty-four-years of being me and I have wonderful skills in listening, organizing, marketing and writing.

I had been out of town for five months and returned last weekend when I saw the write up in Sunday's *Calendar*. I didn't have a ticket but arrived at the museum at 7:00 p.m., was able to buy one at the window and then secure a front row seat, all in about three minutes. Yet the theater had been sold out. It just seems like I was supposed to be there.

I'd love to be able to take you to dinner or lunch. It would be an extraordinary privilege. Please let me know when. Thank you for a lovely evening, Sincerely, Edward J. Funk

 After two or three weeks passed without a response, I assumed that I had hit an impasse and forgot about Loretta Young.

Five months later, I opened my mailbox in the courtyard of my apartment building and found a handwritten letter. It had a Beverly Hills return address which didn't ring any bells. As I opened it while climbing the stairs to my apartment, I realized that it was from Loretta Young! I couldn't believe it! She wrote:

August 30, 89

Dear Mr. Funk, Your charming letter dated March 24th still sits on my desk --waiting to be answered -- so after five months --I shall try.

I have mixed emotions regarding an autobiography-I have discussed it with three of the top publishers in this country. Nothing ever developed because of the kind of book they would like-a tell all book-no way. My agents are William Morris Agency- Mr. Norman Brokaw is my personal representative. I must tell you he is very difficult to deal with. He is the best agent, I believe, in the entire business and is concerned primarily with his client, in this case, Loretta Young.

I really don't know what I'm saying to you-on the one hand I know there is a book, a good book, in me -- on the other, I don't want to join the rat race in order to get it done.

If you'd like to send a Xerox copy of this letter to Mr. Brokaw along with one of your own, I would have no objection-I loved your letter, it was very beautifully written -- Loretta Young

After receiving Loretta's letter, I immediately sat at my computer and wrote Norman Brokaw. I concluded, saying that I would call in a couple of days to firm an appointment. When I did call, his administrative assistant said, "Mr. Funk, Mr. Brokaw received your letter and has already responded to you by mail." I thanked her and hung up. It didn't sound promising.

A few days passed and no letter forthcoming, I called Brokaw's office. Again I spoke with his administrative assistant and this time she said, "Mr. Funk, Mr. Brokaw will meet with you. Miss Young has called requesting that he do so." I had copied her on my initial letter to Norman Brokaw which prompted her to intercede.

This all transpired in August. It would be October before Mr. Brokaw made time to see me. What Loretta had failed to mention in her letter was that in addition to Brokaw being her agent, he was also the CEO of the William Morris Agency. Meeting me was not high on his priority list. Finally, he could fit me in. When I walked into his office, which seemed cavernous at the time, he continued to sit, and pointedly did not invite me to sit down in one of the two winged chairs in front of his desk. Even seated, I observed that he was a well-dressed, well-groomed man, including a fresh manicure. He looked at me with annoyance and said, "Mr. Funk. I'm in touch with the best writers in the world. What is it that you can do that they can't?" I replied, "I can't speak for any other writer. I can only speak for myself." He then asked, "If you were to write this book with Miss Young, what would it be about?" I replied, "I can't answer that either. It's her life. She's going to have to tell me. What I do bring to the effort is that I'm a very good listener and as I listen I'll know what further questions to ask."

That response seemed to interest him mildly. Then he asked, "What have you done?" I knew that this would be the killer question and I responded. "I've written biographies for business people but the idea is the same: get the best story out of the subject that you can." Amazingly, he seemed to allow me to slide with that answer and then he asked, "What else have you done?" I told him about my career in advertising with Sea World and then with The *Queen Mary*. When I mentioned the *Queen Mary*, he asked, "Do you know Monty Livingston?" I did. He was on the board of directors for the Wrather Corporation and was one of two on that board with whom I felt I had a good relationship.

It turned out that Monty Livingston was a good friend of Norman Brokaw and this connection seemed to open the door. No longer was I being interrogated. Mr. Brokaw started sharing with me some of his success stories as an agent and why the collaborations had been successful. He was Bill Cosby's agent and he took a call from Mr. Cosby while I was now comfortably entrenched in one of the winged chairs. Forty minutes passed, and he finally said that it might be interesting for Loretta to meet me. His assistant would call with the details.

That didn't happen right away. It was mid-December before an invitation for afternoon tea at Loretta's home was arranged. The day before, I drove into Beverly Hills to make sure I knew exactly where she lived.

Chapter Three: Meeting Loretta

The following day I arrived a few minutes before the appointed time. I sat in my eleven-year-old Volkswagen Rabbit and did some deep breathing exercises so that I'd appear calm. I was wearing a blue blazer, white shirt, red and blue stripped tie, and grey slacks. I grabbed my brief case, with prepared questions and a tape recorder enclosed, and opened the gates without resistance. I then rang the bell and waited. Finally the door opened and it was Loretta herself, her grayish green eyes signaling a flash of bewilderment. I explained who I was. She said, "Oh, come in, please. I recently lost my secretary and things have been chaotic." I entered the foyer and she continued, "I'll be with you after I freshen my lipstick." She ushered me into the living room and excused herself into a powder room off the foyer.

Loretta joined me momentarily. Her salt and pepper hair was pulled back into a chignon and she was wearing black slacks and a black sweater sporting some small red flowers on the front. I stood as she re-entered the room and she pointed me to a cushioned chair, one of five, placed around a glass table supported by Chinese pedestals. I followed her lead and quickly realized that I wouldn't need my tape recorder or any prepared questions. This was a visit by which she would size me up. My number one goal was to be a good listener.

She walked the length of the large room to select a scrapbook and large envelope. First, we looked at the scrapbook of family pictures starting with one of her, her older sisters and brother Jack, dressed in the role of little nymphs as extras for SIRENS OF THE SEA. She was four or five and it was the second film in which Loretta and her siblings appeared. The remaining pictures were more conventional family fare. It was evident that her mother had been a beauty. I didn't see any pictures of her father that day. Surprisingly there were pictures of John Wayne and his first wife, Josie, and I learned that they had been married in the garden of Loretta's home in 1933. Loretta and the older sisters had known Josie since early adolescence. There were formal pictures of Loretta and her children and the last pages included snapshots of her grown children, her daughters-in-law, and grandchildren. Already I was picking up vibes regarding her feelings toward certain family members: I suspected the more formal her tone, the more ambivalent she was about them.

The envelope contained two dozen or so pictures from her movie and television careers. One very large print was taken for LAUGH, CLOWN, LAUGH, the film during which she turned age fifteen. In the picture, she was lying on her back, her head resting on her long dark curls with her face slightly turned toward the camera. It was her eyes that commanded attention. When I commented on this, she said, "Interesting that you say that. The director, Herbert Brenon, told me that I was selected because of my eyes. I was this skinny little thing but he said that he could pad my body, even pad my legs, but I had the eyes that he wanted." Later, I also noted that she apparently liked pictures of herself when she wasn't directly looking at the camera. Again, she said that I was perceptive, that she thought pictures were more interesting when you weren't looking into the camera.

Some of the pictures had been photographed on specific film sets such as one from RACHEL AND THE STRANGER but the majority were studio publicity stills. Something else I found interesting: she could identify when a picture was taken, either a studio shot or more personal ones by whatever she was wearing. For instance, "That was Peter's (her son) baptism; I remember the white dress."

Going through the scrapbook and the career photos took a couple of hours because each one evoked memories and sometimes the context of those memories was quite extensive. That was fine with me. In the first place, even if my demeanor was calm, underneath, I was churning. I didn't want to say or do anything that would blow this opportunity. And, yes, I was captivated by everything she had to tell me. I had realized shortly after I moved to Southern California that the Hollywood which had cast its spell on me was long gone. Now I was listening to someone who had lived it from the silents, through the golden age of film, into the pioneering days of television. And someone who had lived as a star!

The darkness of an early December evening began creeping into the room. Loretta got up and turned on her Christmas tree which she said she had bought at a charity auction, fully decorated. All the ornaments were either clear-glass, red glass, or white alabaster. There was a cinnamon fragrance in the room but I don't remember any lighted candles.

I asked her. "When you get up in the morning and look into the mirror, do you see that you're beautiful?" She replied very matter of fact, "People continue to tell me that, but I knew when I was beautiful, and I know what I look like today, and I know the difference." I think she realized that the question was sincere and was pleased by it.

Finally she said that she was going out that evening and needed to start dressing. Then she said, "I think we can work together if you can come to terms with Norman." I said that I'd do everything in my power to make that happen. With that she escorted me to the door. A minute later I was in my Rabbit, turning onto Benedict Canyon Drive and shouting with joy.

I met with Norman later that week. We came to an agreement with no formal contract signed. He gave me Loretta's phone number and now it would be up to me to arrange the interview schedule.

Chapter Four: Loretta's Formidable Charm

I've written the story of Loretta's growing-up years in the biography, *Behind the Door: the Real Story of Loretta Young*, but since her sisters were still very much part of Loretta's life in the years I knew her, some background might be helpful. Within the first week, I met Loretta's two older sisters, Polly Ann Hermann and Sally Foster. Both had been actresses. Polly Ann 's friend, character actor, Alan Mowbray, had dubbed her "Queen of Poverty Row" for all the work she did for low budget studios like Monogram. I think her best film available on YouTube is BORDER PATROLMAN with George O'Brien (1936). The second one I'd recommend is THE LAST ALARM (1940)

Sally grew up with the name of Betty Jane; Paramount Studios decided they liked the name Sally Blane better. In addition to Paramount, Sally was under contract to RKO before she, too, drifted into quickie films. A good YouTube movie for Sally is PROBATION (1932). She's beautiful in it and has a lot of screen time. You can see what she looked like six years later in CRASHING THROUGH DANGER (1938). I mention their early careers because the competition that began in the early decades of their lives was still playing out when I walked in.

It's my theory, that even before their film work, the three of them, as well as a younger brother, Jack, and eventually, a younger half-sister, Georgiana, would compete for their mother's love. The father of the four oldest had walked out the door one summer day when Loretta was age four and never came back.

It's also my theory that when one parent abandons the children, particularly young children, on some subconscious level there's a fear that the other parent might abandon them as well.

Their mother, Gladys, a courageous, strong and capable woman, raised her family by managing a succession of Los Angeles boarding houses. She was the center of their lives and they were the center of hers, but she was physically undemonstrative, never hugging or kissing her children. The most she offered was a touch of her hand to their cheek. Gladys had been brought up in a convent boarding school in Kentucky, and her soft southern voice was never raised. Nevertheless, it was what *wasn't* said that held her children in check.

Polly Ann, oldest and most aware of her mother's struggles, became most like her and carried her mother's sense of pragmatism throughout her life. Sally was less than two years younger and she and Polly Ann were best friends. Sally had been her father's favorite and, as far as she was concerned, paid a hefty price for that in her relationship with her mother. Like her father, she said what she thought: not acceptable to Gladys's sense of civilized equanimity. At age four, younger brother Jack was allowed to go live with a wealthy, childless couple and although he was never formally adopted, grew up with the name of Jack Lindley. Georgiana, ten years younger than Loretta, was the only child of Gladys's second marriage to accountant and one time boarder George Belzer. After Gladys's second career as an interior decorator took off, and when she discovered that her second husband had been a womanizer like her first, she divorced him.

As children, Polly Ann and Sally shared everything; Loretta was a loner, living in her own little dream world. She would come to life if there was an opportunity to garner some attention. As Sally recalled, "She wouldn't do a thing to help around the house until she noticed one of the boarders watching, and then she worked her fanny off."

Georgiana was not as present in Loretta's later years. Even though she was just ten years younger than Loretta, she grew up in an entirely different world made possible by her working actress sisters. Also, during the years I knew her, she and husband, actor Ricardo Montalban, lived a busy social life of their own.

Polly Ann lived in a Spanish style home in West Los Angeles, a home previously occupied by singer Mel Torme. She never quite forgave him for a remodeling project that accommodated a pool table at the expense of the breakfast nook off the kitchen. Sally owned a fourplex in Beverly Hills and occupied the two top two-bedroom apartments. All three of the older sisters lived within fifteen minutes of each other.

One thing I had to get used to was the sisters constantly switched names for Loretta and Sally. Sally could be Sally, Bet or Betty Jane. Loretta could be Loretta, Gretchen or Gretch. Gretchen had been her birth name until First National Pictures' silent film star, Colleen Moore, suggested that they name their new contract player "Loretta" after one of her dolls from her famous doll collection.

When I related details of my early meetings with Loretta, a few of my gay pals wanted an in-depth description of her home and everything in it. I had been so focused on Loretta that my description of the house and furnishing failed their expectations by a wide margin. I promised that I'd do better in the weeks ahead.

Later I was able to provide the following: The outside of the house was a three story grey stucco structure with a mansard roof. It looked huge because it was so wide from end to end but when you got inside, you realized that it was like a movie set with very little depth.

There were three things to catch your attention in the foyer. First was a winding staircase with a pewter balustrade. The original builder and occupant of this house had been Sidney Guilaroff, head hairdresser at MGM (it was his decision to make Lucile Ball a redhead). Actresses Debbie Reynolds and Greer Garson gifted Guilaroff the staircase that came out of a Parisian home. It was used as the center point and the rest of the house built around it.

Second, a crystal chandelier hung from the second story through the stairwell and had once belonged to actress Constance Bennett. Years earlier, Loretta had bought Constance Bennett's home and then moved that chandelier from one subsequent home to the next until she settled on Ambassador Avenue.

Third was a Zebra rug. It was something that Loretta's mother had placed when she decorated the home in the late '60s, and now was showing wear. During the weeks before Christmas, there was a little box on a table in the foyer that said "Loretta's Zebra Fund." Loretta explained to me that her family never knew what to get her for Christmas so she put the little box out so they could contribute to replacing her zebra rug. Loretta had had the rug taken up one evening before she had guests but had inadvertently left the little box on the table. The next day she discovered a check from Gloria Stewart, wife of actor James Stewart. She had mistakenly thought that it was a "Save the Zebras Fund." Loretta returned the check.

There was a cloak closet off the foyer. When it was opened, little spot lights shined on two shelves, the top shelf holding Loretta's Best Actress Oscar and the second, her three Best Actress Emmys. Her mother considered displaying the awards gauche and this was her compromise.

The living room was long and narrow, probably fifty feet long and twenty across. A huge window in the rear wall showcased a hanging garden that made the room appear wider. A wading pool visible through double doors at the end of the room also created a perspective of space. There were several paintings, one of Loretta done in pointillism style. Her strategically placed Chinese pieces such as the Ming Dynasty horses situated on the fireplace mantle were sources of pride. Colors of whites, creams, and greens were carried throughout.

A pattern soon emerged once we started working. I arrived at Loretta's home at 2:00 in the afternoon. Loretta was not an early riser. She was often up until the early morning hours and stayed in bed until after 10:00. This allowed her time to dress and attend noon mass at The Church of the Good Shepherd, located a few blocks away. I would stay until 5:30 or 6:00 at which time Loretta would need to start getting ready if she had evening plans. Two or three nights a week she would be going out as "Loretta Young." This didn't mean a public type of appearance; she seldom did that. Rather, she was being invited out to private parties or as a guest to a "name" restaurant because she still had the cache of fame from her movie and television days.

On other nights, Sally or Polly Ann might come for dinner. Loretta didn't cook, didn't know *how* to cook. However, Darlene, a woman about my age, who had entered Loretta's life as a fan and was still around two decades later, prepared meals which she brought over so that all Loretta had to do was heat them in an oven. As I came to know Loretta better, I observed that there were a number of people who entered her life as fans and stayed around because they served her purposes.

I soon realized that Loretta was taking our project very seriously, and the discipline she demonstrated suggested to me how she must have approached her work on film. We took a chronological route to her story, our first days discussing her years of growing up in Los Angeles. She was surrounded by female family members. Brother Jack was out-of-the-picture and her Aunt Collie's husband had run off, leaving her with two young daughters. She and her sister Gladys combined forces and managed neighboring boarding houses.

When we got into her film work as a child extra, I prepared questions based on research I conducted at The Margaret Herrick Library of Motion Pictures Arts and Sciences. I soon discovered why so many of the clerks demonstrated a haughty attitude. They had degrees from film schools like the University of Southern California, but this was as far as their expensive educations had taken them. I remember being there one evening after spending the afternoon at Loretta's when she called the library looking for me. It was a stormy night, and Loretta left a message that I was welcome to stay at her home rather than drive to Long Beach(I chose to go home). I got a little more respect at the library after that.

I remember the first night I met Sally; she had come for dinner. I didn't think she and Loretta looked much alike until I saw her from her left profile and then I noticed a strong resemblance. Sally had tinted her hair red and I think that made her look older. I sensed that these two didn't always get along; Sally's jovial nature that night seemed forced. After dinner, Sally and I were in the living room, and she commented on what great spirits Gretch was in. Then she said, "You know why, don't you? It's all because of you." It was kind of like, "The woman's fallen for you. Don't you get it?"

At times, it did seem that Loretta was courting me as if I was the last male alive. A bit of an exaggeration, I'm sure, but she made sure that I had pillows at my back in the most comfortable chair.

When she realized that I didn't drink alcohol, she found out what chocolates I liked and make sure that they were available. I didn't know quite what to make of it. After all, Loretta in her youth had been chased by movie stars and men of great wealth, millionaires who were the billionaires of their time. I did realize that she wanted me to like her so that I would see her in a positive light. But there was more to it. As time went on, I realized that I was becoming the man in her life, at least for a time. The men she currently went out with were escorts or "suits" as her sister Georgiana would later describe such men. With me it was a new relationship. I was a different kind of man. Not because I was thirty-two years younger, but because I came from both a different and yet similar background. Different in that I came from outside the entertainment world; the same in that she saw our family backgrounds based on the same solid principles. Probably most of all, she took delight in my fascination with her.

It was all a bit heady. For the first six weeks, I think I became lightheaded every time I entered her doors. Although much of the world had forgotten Loretta Young, she was delivering for me the Hollywood of my youthful dreams.

I started sliding into Loretta's life more and more, and when she wasn't going out, she'd often invite me for dinner. If there wasn't a "Darlene" prepared meal, Loretta would open a can of pepper soup, fry a hamburger, and put a salad together. What she did do in the kitchen, she did elegantly. She would skin and de-seed the tomatoes before slicing them for the salad.

One evening we were doing the dishes. She was washing and I was drying. She handed me a plate that didn't pass my inspection and I handed it back. She looked at me askance and with arched eyebrows, said, "Really!" Then she smiled. I don't think, figuratively, many people had handed her back a dish to do over again. I knew at that moment that we were becoming better friends.

The first time I went out with her for an evening was to accompany her to dinner with Sir Daniel Donahue. Dan Donahue became a wealthy man from his wife's estate; she had been an heiress to the Standard Oil of California fortune. The "Sir" came from being knighted by the Vatican, tied to a large donation. What I remember most about that evening was riding in the backseat of his new Jaguar and listening to the conversation between Daniel and Loretta in the front. They were lamenting how people had become so money hungry and that it took their focus off the important things in life. I thought to myself, "Both of these people have Rolls Royces in their garages!"

I also remember Loretta talking about me as if I wasn't sitting in the back. She said, "I'm not sure how this book will turn out but this young man is such a good listener. He's so very sensitive." I think she was right in that I was very sensitive at that time, but what she didn't know was that it flowed from my recent breakdown. By this time I was even grateful for the delay of getting in to see Norman Brokaw and then the delay of meeting Loretta. I still tired easily and would go home exhausted after our working sessions. I was being allowed to heal at a pace that seemed providential.

Chapter Five: Meeting Loretta's Family and Friends

I soon met both of Loretta's sons: Christopher and Peter. They were born eleven months apart and my birthday was right in the middle, making us all around forty-five. Christopher was the older and lived with his wife Linda in Palm Springs, 100 miles east of Los Angeles. Peter, his wife, and two young children lived 100 miles north in Solvang, California. In time, I would sense that the distance geographically was symbolic of their overall relationship.

The circumstances of Loretta's second marriage to Tom Lewis, the father of the boys, may help explain the familial relationships as I observed them. Loretta married Tom in 1940. After six years of tumultuous relationships with men that included Spencer Tracy and Clark Gable, Loretta was seeking stability by marrying a man eleven years older. A never-married Catholic, Tom was a success in his own right. He was in the advertising business at a time when agencies produced most radio shows, and he produced hits such as THE KATE SMITH SHOW. Loretta liked the fact that Tom was not in the film business but close enough to understand it.

It was a marriage built on deception from the beginning. Loretta was marrying a man who would give the appearance of being the senior member of the partnership, making the important decisions for both of them. But Loretta knew that Tom liked living extravagantly and that she'd hold the upper hand as the major moneymaker. Tom's deception was that his attraction to Loretta included his intention to leapfrog from being a radio producer to a film producer via Loretta's connections. That didn't happen. The only film that Tom produced was CAUSE FOR ALARM starring, well, Loretta Young. Tom peaked, when as, Colonel Tom Lewis, he headed Armed Forces Radio during World War II. Returning to the advertising agency after the war, he soon quit over a dispute regarding the redecorating budget for his office. From then on, he busied himself managing Loretta's financial matters and, as his son Chris put it, "He wasn't much of a businessman." While Loretta's career continued to flourish, Tom's self-esteem plunged along with their marriage. Tom increasingly focused on building a relationship between him and the boys but his overt favoritism toward Chris made this an uneasy alliance. At one point, he created the PCT Club: meaning the Peter, Chris, Tom Club, which Peter referred to as the "fucking PCT Club." Loretta and Tom separated in 1956 and divorced in 1969.

Chris and Peter both pursued careers in the entertainment world. Chris and Linda operated their own production company which mainly produced documentaries plus some entertainment movies released directly to video. Peter was a founding member of The Moby Grape, a '60s San Francisco rock band.

My first meeting with Chris and Linda occurred on an evening out hosted by Sir Daniel Donahue. A few days later, I drove to Palm Springs and sat down with Chris around their pool. It was cool enough for Chris to be wearing a jacket and he answered questions thoughtfully. The most interesting answer I recall was when I asked him if he thought his dad was ever happy. He replied, "I don't think being happy was important to Dad. Being recognized as someone important was."

I also drove to Solvang to interview Peter. He was a friendly guy, less restrained than his brother, and frank about the hang-ups of growing up as the son of a famous mother. There was a picture of Loretta and Tyrone Power hanging on the living room wall, taken to promote the film, SECOND HONEYMOON. It was the work of George Hurrell, arguably the silver screen's most heralded photographer.

I had actually met Mr. Hurrell the second week I worked with Loretta. Loretta wanted to replace the photo she sent to fans with something fresh, and she had posed for him a few weeks earlier. I sat at the dining room table with them both. He had finished the photo to his satisfaction but I could tell that he was used to complying with his client's requests. Basically, Loretta wanted <u>all</u> wrinkles to be removed. After Hurrell left, I asked her, "Why don't you leave some small wrinkles in? Your fans know you're not thirty-five anymore, and I think they'd be impressed with how great you look in the same way I'm so impressed." Like the "returning the dish to be rewashed" incident, I think Loretta was surprised at my frankness. She listened politely, but when I saw the picture next, all the wrinkles had disappeared. Not long after, I found a book by Hurrell on a shelf in Loretta's living room, featuring a collection of his most famous portraits. The picture of Loretta and Tyrone was on the cover and inside was the inscription, "Loretta, I chose you for the cover because you're the most beautiful of them all!"

Peter's main focus continued to be his music, and a few weeks after I visited him in Solvang he came down to Los Angeles for a reunion appearance of "The Moby Grape" at a Sunset Strip club. He invited me to join him and I met him at Loretta's house before the performance. Loretta had fried us hamburgers which we ate in the kitchen. After she had stepped out of the room, Peter said to me, "Man, you don't know what a big deal this is! I've been waiting my whole life for my mother to fry me a hamburger!"

I joined him at the club. Not much of a rock music fan, I could still appreciate that this was a special evening for Peter and the rest of "The Moby Grape" as well as for the fans who were nodding their heads in a trance; the music seemingly taking them back to the '60s.

By spring I was comfortable in Loretta's home. I now had my own key to the kitchen door and knew how to disable the alarm before going up the stairs to the second floor. There were more and more evenings when we just hung out, often watching movies. She really didn't enjoy watching her own movies. However she had copies of almost seventy of the ninety eight movies she made, and since I wanted to see them all, sometimes she'd join me. I had seen THE FARMER'S DAUGHER, her Oscar winning film before, but I talked her into watching it with me and she had some interesting commentary. One was about her accent. She had learned to speak with a Swedish accent from Ruth Roberts, the same woman who had taught Ingrid Bergman to lose hers. Half-way through the filming, director Henry Potter told her to ease up on the accent. His thinking was that the audience by that time knew that Loretta could pull it off so it was no longer necessary. Loretta's response, "Yes, and the audience will ask what's wrong with that actress? Half the time she speaks with an accent and half of the time she doesn't. Unh uh. I'm keeping it."

In developing her character's physicality, she stood up and demonstrated how Katie, a Minnesota farm girl, would walk from the street curb to the door of the house. It was deliberate and functional. Then she said, "Now, if I were playing a character who's more sophisticated and out to get a man, I'd walk this way." In demonstrating this, the movement was more undulating, with one leg slightly crossing the other, and at a slower pace. Later, I noticed this walk in the last scene of AND NOW TOMORROW as she approached Alan Ladd (whom she couldn't stand in real life).

Another thing she had conceived in developing the "Katie" character was altering the appearance of her own neck. Much like Audrey Hepburn, Loretta's graceful beauty was accentuated by her long neck. For Katie, Loretta had her shoulders built up to shrink the length of the neck. It was only at the end of the film, the love story culminating, that her familiar long neck comes into view.

Loretta and I spent more and more time together, and I would often drive into Beverly Hills to accompany her for Saturday evening mass at The Church of the Good Shepherd. On one of these occasions, we had driven her Rolls Royce, a vintage 1964 model in brown and taupe tones, the last of the Silver Clouds. She'd recently had it detailed and it was a beauty. Returning home, the car broke down at Lexington Avenue and Benedict Canyon Road. This was the corner where Charo lived, the Latin singer who made a career of not understanding English, and, oops, saying something inappropriate on late night TV. Car phones were just emerging and Loretta didn't have one yet. As she stood beside her Rolls, it was fascinating to watch people screeching their brakes, stopping and competing for who would be allowed to help. If it had been me in my aging VW Rabbit, I would have been barraged by angry honks to get my car out of the way.

Loretta also had a station wagon which was her prime mode of transportation, and when we scooted around town I often drove it. We had a little game we would play. When we were stopped at a light, Loretta would observe the occupants in the next car and then deduce their life story. One afternoon, at the corner of Roxbury and Sunset in Beverly Hills, her assessment was particularly prescient. The car to our right was a creamish-yellow Mercedes coupe convertible with its top up. Occupied by two women, it was the driver of whom Loretta offered an evaluation. What I remember was a woman in her forties, with a nicely featured, yet rather hard-looking face, auburn hair, and wearing a sweater with a fur collar. Loretta assessed the value of the sweater, the coiffure, the jewelry, and, of course, the car, and came up with an instant biography. She said that the woman was recently divorced but that her husband had been married before and that this woman was the cause for that breakup. Then the light changed and the Mercedes sped out in front. Tellingly, the license plate read: "HE PAYS." I think Loretta was so good at this game because observing people in their context had provided her schooling as an actress.

One afternoon, in the early weeks of our interviews, Loretta suggested a possible title for the book. What would I think of *Taste and See*? I thought, "What a bizarre idea!" I was familiar with a religious hymn by that name but what did that have to do with anything! I responded, "That's really interesting. However the publisher makes the marketing decisions; we'll have to wait and see."

Over time, I realized that Loretta's reaction to her fan mail was also wait and see. Once a week a large envelope would arrive from the William Morris Agency. When Loretta was rested, she'd take the time to read the letters and appreciate the sentiments. Other weeks, when she was stressed by other matters, those letters went straight to the trash. She'd lament, "It's been thirty years since the TV show ended. Is this ever going to stop!"

It scared her when fans showed up at the door. This happened a few times while I was there and she'd send me out to get rid of them. A similar thing had happened to Polly Ann. Someone had stopped at her home to have her autograph a publicity picture from the early thirties. I was there a few days later and she said, "Why would someone be interested in some cowboy picture I made sixty years ago? It just doesn't make sense." I was beginning to know Polly Ann well enough to see it through her eyes. She had made those films to earn money, totally detached from the sacredness our culture has assigned toward the movie screen and those who appear on it.

Loretta better understood the fan adoration; in fact she had cultivated it. Now she was applying that same focus to our book. My method of working with Loretta was to sit at the round table in the living room and tape our interviews. If Loretta wanted to discuss something personal, not for public consumption, she'd say, "Turn that thing off." I had a friend, Larry Wilson, a medical transcriber, transcribing these tapes. He did so generously but he needed to be paid and the cost added up. That's why one night, early in our writing effort, I was particularly grateful to Polly Ann. We were having dinner when Loretta came up with the suggestion that I keep the tape recording running in case anyone said anything interesting. Polly Ann chimed in, "Gretch, that's asking too much. It takes time and money to transcribe those tapes. What we have to say to each other isn't that interesting." I was relieved. It would have been time and money probably not best spent. Loretta's reaction was worthy of note. She said, "I guess you're right," and I got the impression that when Polly Ann did offer a rare chastisement, it was taken seriously. Months later Polly Ann would tell me that all she had to do was give Loretta a "look" and she would fall in line. I suspected that it was the same "look" that Gladys had used on her children. When I first met Polly Ann she was near 80, and although still attractive, looked her age. Her voice was deep, altered by decades of smoking.

The first meeting with Georgiana and Ricardo Montalban came unplanned. Loretta and I were eating in a Japanese restaurant in

Century City and the Montalbans were dining there as well. They invited us to join them. Ricardo was appearing in a Los Angeles production of DON JUAN IN HELL along with Stewart Granger and David Carradine. He was venting his frustrations that neither of those actors was able to remember their lines. Complicating the matter, they missed different lines with each performance, so Ricardo was worn out trying to hold the play together. I was fascinated by his laments, but on the way home Loretta expressed the opinion that Ricardo's ego monopolized the evening's conversation. This fascinated me because Loretta had demonstrated on other occasions her own ability to hold forth. It wasn't so easy seeing it in herself.

Josie Wayne, John Wayne's first wife, was the same age as Polly Ann. It was the friendship between the two of them as adolescents that introduced Josie into the household. She and Loretta became closer friends in their adult years as they traveled in the same circles. Josie came to Loretta's one day to allow me to interview her. She was blonde, vivacious, and a flirt. In fact, she was telling me a story about some woman, and to describe her, said, "She's the kind of a woman who lost interest in men a long time ago," and then she looked to Loretta and said, "You know what I mean." Loretta nodded her head in affirmation and I thought to myself, "What an interesting observation! And I'm certainly in the presence of two woman who have not lost their interest in men." They were still playful and coquettish.

During the conversation that afternoon, Loretta brought up the point that even though they had been best friends all these years, they still maintained certain boundaries. For instance, she said, "When Josie and Duke were still married, and he was having an affair with Marlene Dietrich, I didn't go and blab about that to Josie." An uncomfortable look crossed Josie's face even though the John Wayne/Marlene Dietrich fling was fifty years in the past.

Irene Dunne was one of Loretta's closest movie star friends. I never met Irene, but one day I answered Loretta's phone and it was she calling. Identifying herself as Mrs. Griffith, she sounded peeved that she was talking to a stranger. This was only a few months before she died, and Loretta was visiting her weekly. I gave Loretta the message and she called her back. Then Loretta related a conversation with Irene a few months earlier. "I tried to get over to see her every week and call her every day. One time I called, after being out of town, and told her, "Irene, I love you." She said, 'No you don't! You haven't called me in two weeks.' Oh, the tone in her voice, like a hurt, angry child. I felt so guilty and I was determined I'd make up for it. But, strangely enough, for her to say that to me was very touching. It was the nearest she ever came to telling me that I meant something to her. Throughout her life, Irene has never shown her feelings and now the wall had come down."

In the last week of Irene's life, I went with Loretta to her home as we were en route someplace else. Loretta ran upstairs to see Irene while I waited downstairs. By that time, I understood that Irene was dying and it was eerie to be in her home. It was a formal house; the door was actually opened by an elderly butler in uniform. As Loretta climbed the stairs, he ushered me into the living room and disappeared. I knew that Gladys, Loretta's mother, had decorated the home. It had much the same feel as Loretta's, only tired, a bit thread-bare, with a feel as if no one had been in these rooms for a long time. The house seemed to know that its mistress was dying.

Chapter Six: Mixing with the Really Rich and Famous

I had already become one of Loretta's frequent escorts. She told me she was confident I would conduct myself well, especially since I didn't drink and wouldn't say something either of us might regret. One such occasion was the christening of triplets. The grandmother, Fiorenza Courtright, the widow of the man who managed the Beverly Hills Hotel, was hosting. The babies' father was a grandson of George Halas, the Chicago Bears titan. It was a Sunday afternoon affair and most of the women were wearing white. Loretta and I sat down with Jane Wyman who was still starring in TV's FALCON CREST. She was telling Loretta about the difficulties she was having with the director and other actors. Loretta shook her head and said, "It's just ridiculous. Don't they realize that they're going to have to do it your way in the end?" Jane agreed. The conversation was enlightening to me regarding the power these actresses were used to wielding.

Actress/dancer Ann Miller was also there. She seemed nervous, as if out of her element.

Shortly thereafter I escorted Loretta to a much larger affair at the home of billionaire Marvin Davis. He made his fortune mainly in oil but also owned 20th Century -Fox and The Denver Broncos for periods of time. Since this was an event when Loretta played "Loretta Young," we arrived in the Rolls Royce with me at the wheel. Security was elaborate. After stopping at the gate, guards looked underneath the car to make sure that no one was holding on. Then I was instructed to drive slowly enough for men to walk along the sides of the car until we reached the entrance which initially wasn't in sight. Upon arriving, Mr. Davis, a very large man, at least three hundred pounds, greeted us at the entrance. There were two white, standard poodles trained to be immobile, sitting on each of his sides. As we entered the house's rotunda Mrs. Barbara Davis welcomed us. Beyond was a large salon where the other guests were mingling. As we walked in, Loretta spotted Kirk Douglas standing with another man. She stopped and said, "Kirk, you know Ed Funk," and then she waltzed off to speak to someone on her own. Well, of course Kirk Douglas did not know Ed Funk and he just stared at me. Feeling uncomfortable, I smiled and walked away. Later I realized that Kirk Douglas had had a recent stroke and was in the process of regaining his ability to speak. I caught up with Loretta long enough for her to walk past Merv Griffin, saying, "Merv, you know Ed Funk," and she was off again. Merv, too, was in motion but smiled and said hello.

I set a goal to become as inconspicuous as possible which would require striking up a conversation whenever I saw someone unengaged. I also noted that there were several good-looking men who appeared to be by themselves. I wondered if they might be gay. I then turned to find the next person to talk with, and facing me less than a foot away was Ronald Reagan. Being practically on top of each other, a conversation ensued. I introduced myself, a formality he didn't need to reciprocate. I told him that I had heard him speak in Orlando where he was campaigning for his first term. The venue was a Sea World outdoor arena. He asked, "Was it a good speech?" I responded, "Of course." I asked him what that was like, flying from city to city, giving the speech several times a day. He replied, "You know what city you're in at the time, but if someone asked me the next day where had I been the day before, it would have been tough to remember." Then he smiled, turned and walked away. He seemed slightly bored and I had the impression that he had been dragged to this affair by Nancy. I wondered how many dress-up parties he had suffered through the decades. I also realized that the attractive men I spotted were the Secret service roaming the room and that the security at the Davis property that evening must have been enhanced by Secret Service protocols.

Once again, I caught up with Loretta and this time she introduced me to Nancy Reagan and her pal, Betsy Bloomingdale. Again, Loretta didn't give any specifics as to who I was and was soon off on her own once again. My next attempt at conversation was with Eva Gabor. I could tell that she was fun, so I said, "When I listen to you, you sound just like Eva Gabor. " She laughed and said, "I know what you mean. When I first came to Hollywood and met Cary Grant, he sounded just like Cary Grant."

When it was time to move on from that conversation, I spotted Michael Eisner, head of the Walt Disney Corporation, and his wife. As soon as I approached them, he immediately looked over my shoulder to see if there was someone more interesting and was off. His wife was kinder and we had a nice visit. Two things that I remember her saying was how grateful they were for her husband's tremendous success and that they didn't allow their children to watch television, interesting because Disney owned ABC.

I couldn't help noticing Nancy Reagan because she would glide by me and, while smiling, give me a quizzical look that asked, "Who are you and what are you to Loretta?" I could only smile back. I noticed that she was wearing a black "baby doll" type dress, thin straps over the shoulders with a flared skirt ending above the knee.

I was relieved when the butler gonged a chime to announce dinner because I had already checked out the tables in the dining room and knew that I'd be sitting next to Loretta. Nancy Reagan and Betsy Bloomingdale were the first in and Loretta and I followed. When no one else ensued, the two of them left the room, apparently uncomfortable at being the first ones. This gave me the opportunity to say to Loretta, "Nancy Reagan's head looks too big for her body." She replied, "Actually, her body is too small for her head. I imagine that she's dieted down to a point where she's out of proportion. Also, if she were a vain old movie star like me, she'd have floor to ceiling mirrors to see what she looks like head to toe. My guess is that she does her hair and makeup sitting at a dressing table. Just seeing her head and shoulders, she doesn't realize how out of proportion she looks." I suspected Loretta was right on both counts. The dieting down theory was supported by the fact that Mrs. Reagan's legs were not her best feature. Piano legs in appearance, she should have skipped the "baby doll" look.

Soon, everyone arrived in the dining room. A very weary looking Dinah Shore, wearing a white pants suit, was sitting at the same table with us. I wondered if she was ill. Right next to me was Harriet Deutsch, wife of Armand Deutsch, a film producer who had grown up in a wealthy Chicago family. He claimed to have been Leopold and Loeb's intended victim, in 1929, for their quest to commit the perfect murder. Deutsch was spared because he had a scheduled dentist appointment that day and was met at school by his grandfather's chauffeur.

Mrs. Deutsch was an attractive blonde. In the course of the conversation she mentioned recently spotting Loretta's sister, Polly Ann, and was shocked at how old she allowed herself to look. I wanted to say, "Look, the woman's eighty. Why can't she look eighty?" but I knew, by this time, that the most grievous sin in Beverly Hills was growing old.

Sidney Poitier came to our table and he and Loretta repeated to each other "I love you" a number of times, using guttural voices fitting a mating call. Very strange.

Loretta's introduction, "You know Ed Funk," did fool one person. We were leaving the party the same time as Merv Griffin and he said to me in a friendly voice, "Good to see you, again, Ed."

I was to see the Reagans again soon thereafter. The occasion was a rededication of the Motion Picture Retirement Home in Woodland Hills, CA. Loretta, Ronald Reagan, and Robert Young, had all been part of the dedication of the Motion Picture Hospital in 1948, and the three of them were present again. The day got off to a bumpy start. Loretta and I were to accompany Josie Wayne, her oldest son, Michael, and his wife, Gretchen. I arrived at Loretta's just as the Waynes were arriving in a limousine. I had met Michael before when I interviewed him at his office;

Loretta was his godmother. Having a key to the kitchen I announced that I'd let myself in and tell Loretta we had all arrived. The house was stone quiet and Loretta didn't answer when I called up the stairway. I opened the front door and Michael entered. I assured him that I knew the code to turn off the alarm so that we could go upstairs and check on Loretta. I must have pushed the wrong numbers because the alarm started blasting and Michael gave me a disgusted look. I don't think I ever recovered in his esteem. The alarm had awakened Loretta and she prevented any further repercussions by calling the security company. It was the fastest that I would ever know her to dress and we were soon on our way to Woodland Hills.

One of the residents was actress Mae Clark whom Loretta and I went to visit. She was the actress in whose face Jimmy Cagney famously smashed a grapefruit in THE PUBLIC ENEMY. Mae had told Loretta the script originally called for Cagney to rub eggs into her face and that Cagney refused to do that. It was Mae who came up with the idea of the grapefruit. Either way, Loretta always felt that the scene of macho aggressiveness had ruined Mae Clark's career. Loretta employed Mae when she could. She appeared in a late Loretta film, BECAUSE OF YOU, as well as several of her television episodes.

There were many celebrities wandering around the grounds that day such as Roddy McDowall, Robert Wagner and his wife Jill St. John. I was taking a good look at Jill St. John. She was wearing a tomato red suit and it looked great with her red hair. A woman, noticing my focus, sidled next to me and said, "Poor Jill, she used to be so beautiful." Meoooww.

A band played "Hail to the Chief" when the Reagans arrived. That surprised me since he was no longer President, but it did catch everyone's attention and the former President and Mrs. Reagan swept through the crowd and onto a platform. Loretta and Robert Young also joined them. Ronald Reagan said some quick, pithy words and then the Reagans were swept back to their waiting car.

We soon left as well and Michael Wayne hosted us for a late lunch at the Hillcrest Country Club. A lot of the conversation was about John Ford. He directed many of John Wayne's greatest films but Michael continuously made the point that Ford was a real bastard. Loretta had worked with Ford and concurred. Only Josie's take was different. When her kids were still living at home, someone anonymously sent her flowers every Easter. One year she sent one of the boys to chase down the delivery man and ferret out the name of her secret admirer. It was John Ford.

A fan approached the table and asked Loretta for an autograph. Her reply was, "Not now, I'm with friends." Michael had pointed out in my interview with him a few weeks earlier how Loretta and his father handled that situation in their own ways. John Wayne always took the time to sign an autograph because he felt he owed it to the people who bought movie tickets and made him a star.

The Waynes dropped us off at Loretta's and after entering the house through the kitchen, Loretta pressed the flashing message button on her phone. Once she realized who it was, she rolled her eyes and held the receiver out so that I could hear. It was Nancy Reagan, scolding Loretta for never returning her phone calls. She was calling to invite Loretta for a dinner she was hosting for actress Claudette Colbert. I found it ironic to discover that Loretta had been dodging Nancy Reagan's phone calls having just seen the Reagans regaled like royalty a few hours earlier.

Loretta changed her clothes and when she returned, I said, "With all the celebrities present today, the photographers seemed most interested in you." She smiled and said, "I can tell you one reason. When I finally got up this morning, knowing that it was going to be a hot day, I knew that most women would be wearing white because it's cooler. I decided to wear black and not just a black dress but a big black hat as well. I couldn't help but stand out." It had been a long time since Loretta's movie star days, but she still thought like one.

Then she told me a story about another black hat. Director Mervyn Leroy had been integral in the hiring of Loretta as a young teen at First National Studios. When he died she attended his funeral. The service received national news coverage, and Loretta was shown wearing a black hat. A few weeks later, she received a call from then First Lady Nancy Reagan. Nancy made small talk but then the conversation eventually led to her seeing the coverage of Loretta at Leroy's funeral. Loretta told me at that point she knew where the conversation would head. And she was right, Nancy wanted to know who the hat maker was.

Loretta and Ronald Reagan were invited to participate in another rededication. Warner Brothers had re-acquired some soundstages that had originally fallen into their hands when they purchased First National Pictures in 1928. Warner Brothers had been Reagan's major home studio and one of three for Loretta during her long film career. The evening was to be a big event and for Loretta to participate would require more than a phone call. As I would learn, her mode was to invite business people to tea; in other words, they had to come to her. The event producers were Bob Daly, Chairman of the Board and Chief Operating Officer of Warner Brothers (who then lived in a Holmby Hills home that Loretta once owned and occupied) and Jack Haley, Jr. Haley had produced the first two THAT'S ENTERTAINMENT series of compilations of MGM musicals. By this time, he was also an ex-husband of Liza Minnelli. Loretta had invited me to the tea as well. Their pitch included showing a clip of eighteen-year-old Loretta that they'd screen at the rededication from I LIKE YOUR NERVE (1931), one of six movies Loretta made with Douglas Fairbanks, Jr. Fairbanks would also be attending the event.

Loretta agreed to introduce a segment of the program. While I was not invited as her escort, she did invite me to accompany her to Warner Brothers for the rehearsal. The studio sent a limousine, a black limousine, as Loretta thought white ones common. After we entered the gates, she pointed to a low one-story building and recalled that it had been used for dressing rooms when she went under contract to First National. Then she related the story about a silent screen star vacating her dressing room when her contract wasn't renewed. Loretta immediately moved her belongings from a dressing room she shared with other contract players into the vacant star dressing room. Her thinking was that she wanted to be a big star, so why not move into a big star's dressing room? When Al Rockett, head of First National, found out he called Loretta to his office. Very gently he informed her he believed she would become a big star, but she was not there yet and, for the time being, she'd have to return to the communal dressing room.

When we arrived at the soundstage where the event was to be held, Loretta was shown through her paces. I noticed again something that I had observed earlier at her home. Event Producers Bob Daley and Jack Haley, Jr. treated Loretta with kid gloves, very careful not to say the wrong thing. Apparently, Loretta had a reputation for being temperamental that had lived on long after her career was over. Also, Loretta didn't seem eager to put them at ease. I hadn't seen this side of her before.

When the event was over she had two interesting tidbits to share. First, she had been seated at a table with the Reagans as well as George Lukas and his date, Debra Winger. At one point, Debra Winger silently summoned a photographer, and while the Reagans weren't looking, had her picture taken with her tongue sticking out at the former President. Loretta wasn't a big fan of Reagan as President but she thought this quite undignified. On a more positive note there was a point when she was descending some steps and Clint Eastwood came to offer his hand. He told her, "You look perfectly lovely tonight," and it made her evening.

As I got to know Loretta better, I also better understood her motivation to dress up and go out so many evenings. It was the dressing up, itself. Loretta never lost her fascination with clothes. During her heyday she was on the "Best Dressed" list so often that they finally deemed her "Best Dressed Emeritus." Generally, she attended small gatherings and was informed prior to the event who else was on the guest list. This was important in that she didn't want to be seen in the same outfit twice. She was a skilled seamstress and often redid her outfits so that they would appear new and fresh.

Loretta also enjoyed the process of preparing to go out. Before describing this procedure, I need to describe the layout of her bedroom suite. There was the bedroom itself with pale blue and silver silk wall covering and an ornate black iron bedstead that originated from an Italian villa. Also in that room was a sitting area the size of a small living room. Leading into the bedroom was an anteroom lined with closets. There was a table in the center where she did her sewing. Her bathroom and a dressing room also entered off of this room. She would take a long soak in the tub before proceeding to the dressing room which was full of windows and mirrors. The windows faced south and Loretta preferred putting her makeup on early enough in the evening so that she would use only natural light. The mirrors were floor length, as she described them when she was assessing Nancy Reagan's grooming woes.

An open stairway to the third floor was on the back wall of the anteroom. Basically, the third floor was one giant storage area for Loretta's gowns, hung on racks like one would encounter in a very upscale store. These dresses weren't a collection from the distant past; she cleared out the inventory now and then by giving them to family and friends (although Polly Ann commented to me that Loretta usually waited one or two seasons too long for this generosity). Many of Loretta's gowns were designed by Jimmy Galanos. A renowned courtier, Galanos was Nancy Reagan's designer of choice when she was in the White House. Jean Louis was Columbia Studios named courtier and gave Jimmy a break early in his career by hiring him as a sketch artist. In turn, Galanos was very generous to Loretta because of her long and close friendship with Jean Louis. Loretta and Jean's relationship had taken many twists and turns with the sharpest curves yet to come.

Chapter Seven: Loretta Breaks her Silence on Gable

Loretta met Jean Louis when he designed her wardrobe for the 1952 film PAULA. Then she and Jean, as well as Jean's soon-to-be wife, Maggie, drifted into a very close friendship that lasted the next thirty-seven years. The former Maggie Fisher, Jean's second wife, was an ex-model who enjoyed playing dress up as much as Loretta. Of course, Loretta provided an entrée to many social occasions but so did the Louises. They owned various homes over the years located in swank neighborhoods: Malibu, California; Palm Beach, Florida; Paris, France, and Montecito, adjacent to Santa Barbara, California, all of which extended their social reach. This was perfect for Loretta. As a divorced Catholic, Loretta's marriage to Tom Lewis was still valid in the eyes of her church as long as Tom lived. Loretta was quite comfortable as the third party attached to Jean and Maggie. Before going out the two women would dress and then present themselves to Jean who would assess their appearance, often appraising that less, as in jewelry, was more. One time he told them to return upstairs and switch dresses which they did, unquestioningly.

I never met Maggie Louis. She died during the two-month-period between my meeting Norman Brokaw in October and Loretta in December. That's why Loretta was unavailable; she was spending most of her time with the Louises in Montecito. The day after Maggie died, the mortuary asked if he wanted to preview how they prepared Maggie. Jean didn't have the stomach so Loretta went. When she saw Maggie's lips made up very prim and tight, Loretta exclaimed, "Oh no, Maggie had full, voluptuous lips. Get me the lip pencil that you used and I'll do it." But Loretta further recalled, "He gave it to me and I started to do it and then stopped. I wasn't prepared for the sensation of her lips being rock hard. Anyway, I finished it and she looked much more like Maggie."

Also, when Loretta had explained to me on that first day, that she had been without a secretary, he was, in fact, dying from complications of AIDS. So when I entered the picture, Loretta had a lot of catching up in her personal life. One task was to complete a 1990 census form. I told her that I'd fill it out if she'd just answer the questions. When the question arose: "How many children have you given birth?" Loretta shouted, "That's none of their damn business," and that brought work on the census to an end.

I was pretty sure I knew what was behind that explosion. Even in Kentland, Indiana, I was aware of rumors that Loretta had given birth to a secret baby fathered by Clark Gable, and then raised the child as her "adopted" daughter.

I didn't know how I was going to approach that topic. As it turned out, Loretta brought it up herself. We had already spent a day discussing various anecdotes related to the Washington State location shooting for CALL OF THE WILD, a 1935 film in which she co-starred with Gable. We were about to end the second day's discussions when Loretta sprang up and, with her normally controlled voice rising, said, "You haven't asked me. You haven't asked me about Clark Gable and Judy." I can still see her pacing the room, wearing a cream colored sweater and matching wool slacks. She was like a caged animal, a cage constructed by fifty-five years of refusing to directly acknowledge the matter, or face her inherent feelings. In our discussions earlier that day and the previous one, she described the flirtatious relationship between her twenty-two-year-old self and the thirty-four-year-old, married Gable. She and her chaperone, Frances Early, shared a room while they were on location. On the train returning to Los Angeles, she occupied her own compartment and that was when Gable arrived, uninvited. Using Loretta's word, he became very "persistent" (Several years later, Loretta used another term to describe this encounter: date rape). That was the only time they had sex.

Over time I slowly learned of Loretta's limited relationship with Gable after she knew she was pregnant, as well as how she managed to have a secret baby. Again, those stories are part of my biography of Loretta. But back to the day of Loretta's initial revelation, she continued pacing as she said her piece. Her composure was uncharacteristically ruffled and her speech pressured. There was a silent pause as she walked toward the end of the room and then she said, "I'm sorry, but I have to think of myself first. You can't put any of this in a book."

I said that I understood, even though I didn't. What did she mean by "thinking of myself first?" I was glad that evening shadows were filling the room because they provided cover to gather my things and leave. All the way home, and into the evening, I thought about, "I'm sorry, but I have to think of myself first." Then I recalled earlier when Loretta discussed one of the consequences of her impulsive decision to elope with actor

Grant Withers just two weeks after her seventeenth birthday. Grant had been married previously and divorced, so marrying him in the Catholic Church was not an option. Father Ward was a young priest whom Gladys engineered into her actress daughters' lives by having him for dinner every Thursday. After her elopement with Grant Withers, Loretta quoted Father Ward as saying, "'You cannot be a movie star and go around behaving as if you are little Jane Doe and have nobody paying attention to you. Everything you do is going to be noted and it is going to be judged. So better a stone be tied around your neck and dropped to the bottom of the ocean than if you give a bad example. And you have already done it to two young girls I know. Two sixteen-year-old Catholic girls have been married out of the Church. You know what each of them said to me? 'Well, Loretta Young's Catholic and if she can do it, I can do it.' Those sins are on your soul. So decide now whether you want to be an actress and behave yourself or not. It can be done. Other people have done it.'"

By this time I knew Loretta well enough to realize that she had held onto her pre-Vatican II Catholicism (which was stricter). I recalled growing up Catholic in the '50s that sex was never discussed, but, somehow you knew that engaging in pre-marital sexual intercourse ranked just slightly below committing murder. (I'm kidding of course… but not completely). I don't think Loretta ever recovered from her guilt of having a baby outside of marriage. The sexual revolution of the '60s, well entrenched by the time I met her, had not altered her thinking. The off-stated quote, "The truth will set you free," did not resonate with her. Rather her position seemed to be, "Never acknowledged, never happened."

I wrote her a letter a few days later suggesting a way that we could acknowledge the Judy/Clark Gable saga without exploiting it. She responded with a letter:

June 15th, 1990

Dearest Ed, I loved your letter of June 11th. I feel gratitude to God for your insight regarding me but I find I cannot put it into writing, for strangers, especially publishers to read. Don't ask me why – I don't know – and I don't remember words – I just remember my feelings of gratitude – of pride in you, my friend – not the author of a book on me. I'm sorry if this doesn't make sense, it's the best I can do – I pray you'll understand. Love as always, Loretta

Not long after the Judy revelation, Loretta invited me to travel with her to Montecito and help her sort through Maggie's clothes. Jean had been in Paris for much of the time since Maggie's death, and Loretta wanted to clear out Maggie's things to make his return easier. Being a natural busy body, I found it interesting opening other people's drawers and taking inventory. I was quite moved by all the little notes I found in both Jean and Maggie's handwriting, basically, "I love you," notes expressed in various ways. That made it all the more astounding when Loretta related that the Louises' relationship had been a platonic one. Maggie had confided in Loretta that she and Jean had sex only one time. Years passed and Maggie asked Jean if they would ever have sex again. Jean's response was, "I don't know." They never did. Hearing this confirmed my conviction that there are all kinds of love stories, that people fulfill each other's needs in various ways.

One day, Loretta wanted to show me the Santa Barbara Mission. I had seen it before but didn't say so. Before we got out of the car we were talking about the chronology of a film she had made and I attempted to place it in time by saying, "That was after Judy was born." Loretta froze. She said, not in an unkind way, but quite deliberately, "Watch what you're saying." My first thought was, "This is absolutely nuts. We're in a closed car with no one around us. Who could possibly hear us?" But then I saw it in a different perspective: holding this secret so tight caused a reflex in Loretta that was irrational. The way it had remained only a rumor and not a confirmed fact was due to her absolute refusal to discuss it with anyone.

This "solid wall of silence" theory of Loretta's would be confirmed for me in the months ahead by a variety of sources. Loretta herself told me that she had never discussed it with Tom Lewis in the sixteen years they lived as husband and wife. Josie Wayne also told me that the subject was never broached between them even though she had known the truth of the matter before Judy was born. Polly Ann told me that the topic had not been addressed among the three older sisters since Judy's wedding. At that time it was Gladys's opinion that Judy should know the facts; Polly Ann and Sally concurred but Loretta issued a strong veto. Loretta had told me that, even though twelve-year-old Georgiana was living in the same house, she had been unaware of Loretta's pregnancy. Georgiana told me that she had known all along but, throughout their entire lives, the subject was never discussed. To me, all of these were examples of Loretta's theorem that if something is not acknowledged, it never happened.

I had traveled to Montecito on Loretta-related business prior to helping pack Maggie Louis's things. Loretta had outlived almost all of her male co-stars. One exception was Robert Mitchum with whom she appeared in 1948's RACHEL AND THE STRANGER. Loretta and Mitchum had remained friends over the decades and she called him to arrange an interview. I prepared as well as I could, mainly researching the film's production history. The day before my appointment with Mitchum, there was an interview with Barbara Walters in *The Los Angeles Times*. She was asked to identify her toughest interviews. She mentioned two: one, a rock star whose name I don't recall, and the other, Robert Mitchum. I immediately felt a pit in my stomach. What was I walking into?

The next day, as I traveled north on California Highway 101, I stopped at a banana plantation I had passed many times before. I purchased some exotic varieties, thinking that if I brought an unusual gift, my introduction might go smoother. When I arrived, Mrs. Mitchum answered the door. I introduced myself and handed her the bananas. She tossed them into a bowl with other fruit and that was that. I had entered through the kitchen door which reminded me of the informality of homes I knew in my youth. Calling out for her husband only added to it. A few seconds later, Robert Mitchum was standing before me. We shook hands and then he asked me to follow him back to his den.

The Mitchum home was quite nice, but I sensed immediately that they prioritized comfort and utility over décor. For instance, as I passed through the dining room, I noticed that it was lined with over-loaded bookshelves. I asked Mitchum, "Who reads all these books?" He replied, "Dorothy, my wife."

His den also had crowded bookshelves, as well as piles of paper that gave it the lived-in look that I had observed through the house. We sat down and started talking about filming RACHEL AND THE STRANGER. Norman Foster, Sally's husband and Loretta's brother-in-law, was the director but Mitchum actually thought Loretta was the producer. He recalled, "She was very knowledgeable about all the backstage work and the cameras and lighting. I suppose it's personal thrift; she just doesn't want to have to do it again." He summed up the working relationship between Loretta and Norman Foster by saying, "He was very, very, conscious, acutely conscious, of her approval or disapproval."

Mitchum offered a personal insight to Loretta. "She projects a serenity and she is in control of herself, or at least gives the impression that she's in control of her circumstances. That control is her armor. I should imagine the reason she keeps herself so collected is because she's so vulnerable. Every once in a while, if things weren't going right, you'd see that vulnerability. Rather than see a temper fly, she might become tearful."

He also made the comment that Loretta was "as big as any of them, right up there with Bette and Joan," meaning Bette Davis and Joan Crawford. As enamored as I was with Loretta and her long-lasting career, I knew better. She may have made more films than either, but they weren't as memorable.

As I became more comfortable with Robert Mitchum, I brought up the interview in the previous day's *The Los Angeles Times* with Barbara Walters. I asked him why he had been so hard on her. He replied, "She asks dumb questions."

While we were having our discussion, Mitchum took a call from Martin Scorsese. Mitchum had appeared as a malicious antagonist to Gregory Peck's good guy in the original CAPE FEAR, and he had agreed to do a cameo in the remake. I asked him what it was like to play evil characters. He responded, "You know, I've made, I think now it's over 200 films. I only played heavies in two, CAPE FEAR and NIGHT OF THE HUNTER, yet those are the performances people remember."

I felt that the interview had gone well but was totally surprised when Mitchum asked me if I'd like to have lunch with him a few days later. Of course I said yes. When I arrived at his home, before he came into the kitchen to join me, I had the opportunity to ask Mrs. Mitchum who read all the books stacked throughout the house. She said, "Bob."

Then he appeared and we were off; it would be his treat but he suggested that I drive. We went to an upscale Mexican restaurant and had a leisurely lunch, leisurely enough for Mitchum to have three double margaritas. The motivation behind the invitation was now apparent; he was supposed to be on the wagon. I wasn't his keeper so I just enjoyed his company.

With his lizard-like eyes and deep voice, he looked and sounded like Robert Mitchum except that he spoke with a vocabulary that belied the tough guy image from his films. I remember him referring to someone as a "nosey parker," a term straight out of an English mystery story. We also talked about other actors. He asked me who I thought was admirable and I said, "Richard Burton." He said, "Do you think so? Anybody could do that voice. It's just a trick," and then he proceeded to speak like Burton. Later, he did a very impressive Charles Laughton. I asked him whom he admired as an actor and he said, "Oscar Homolka." That surprised me. I remembered Homolka from Hitchcock's 1936 British film SABOTAGE but his was hardly a household name.

In the months ahead, I would see more of Robert and Dorothy Mitchum in the capacity of Loretta's escort. Montecito was money, both old and new, and the Mitchums attempted to mix both at a large party celebrating their anniversary. I was seated next to the young wife of a multi-married scion of a company that Sinclair Lewis might have written about. This woman was a new mother and said she planned to write a book on child rearing. I asked her what insights she would share. "Well," she replied, "the most important thing is to hire a French nanny." I thought to myself that the market for her book might be fairly narrow. Also, at that party, I had a conversation with actor Stuart Whitman. When I told him that I was working on a book with Loretta he quoted director William Wellman as saying, "No one in Hollywood broke more hearts than that little Catholic girl, Loretta Young."

I was in even headier company when I escorted Loretta to a party at the residence of Princess Shams Pahlavi. She was the older sister of the late Shah of Iran. In fact the party was a celebration of the Shah's birthday which seemed odd since he was dead. The Princess had a huge home in Beverly Hills, very '60s looking, with white stucco and lots of glass on the outside, white walls also on the inside, but strong accent colors of purples and reds.

Upon entering, Princess Shams appeared to be propped up by some unseen object below her gown and she greeted guests in a ghost like fashion. She didn't move; nothing in her face moved; it was so tight that I don't think anything could, except for her eyes. I had been observing others as she greeted them and they were doing the one cheek/then the other cheek kiss/kiss. When it was my turn, I kissed one cheek and immediately knew that something was wrong. Princess Shams's face became even more frozen, including the eyes. Apparently, one did not allow his lips to actually touch the royal cheek. Nothing was said, and I maintained an appropriate distance for the kiss to the other cheek.

Loretta was seated at one table and I was at another, an arrangement I was getting used to. Usually Loretta was in more august company. I found my place card and sat down. Of course I didn't know anyone, but the other guests were engaged with each other, so I was looking forward to whoever would appear at the empty chair to my left. In a moment or two an older, well-dressed woman materialized and I stood to get her chair. As she seated, she said to me, "Hello, I'm Princess Fawzia of Egypt."

What was I to say? "Hello, I'm Edward of Kentland?" I simply introduced myself and asked if King Farouk had been her brother. She answered yes. Right away I knew more about her family than I'm sure she realized. Loretta had a beautiful emerald necklace with matching earrings that had belonged to King Farouk's mother but were sold when cash ran short. As it turned out, Princess Fawzia was very pleasant company. She spoke of a son, Hussain, who was living in Paris and recently experienced some tough times but was on the rebound. Her sharing something so intimate made me like her all the more. It wasn't until years later when I was reading something, and her name appeared, that I realized that not only was she an Egyptian princess but had also been the first wife of the Shah of Iran.

There was a retired diplomat at our table. When he realized that I was working on a book with Loretta Young he told me that she had been very popular in Middle Eastern countries. He said this was because, unlike many American film actresses, Loretta conveyed a graciousness that was more in sync with their sensibilities.

The lack of graciousness was noted during an evening I spent with Loretta, Polly Ann, and Sally, watching an Academy Award Presentation. They observed that the actresses didn't know how to move in their gowns. Rhetorically, Loretta asked, "Who would teach them?" Then they discussed how the studios of their day paid attention to such matters.

Loretta was a voting member of the Academy. As an actress, she could vote on the acting awards as well as Best Picture. Early in our acquaintance I accompanied her to see MY LEFT FOOT at one of the theaters in the Century City Mall. We were coming down an escalator from the garage and someone standing in line looked up and spotted Loretta. Within seconds everyone in line had turned and, as we got off the escalator, a pathway opened straight to the ticket window, much like the Red Sea parting. We then picked up complimentary tickets available for voting members. I don't know if the people who cleared the way recognized Loretta, or if they just knew that she was someone who had been someone. Loretta had a way of making an entrance when the mood struck her.

The following year we went to see Kevin Costner in DANCING WITH WOLVES. On the way home, Loretta said, I don't need to see the other nominated films or actors, I'm voting everything for DANCING WITH WOLVES, and she did. Ever since then, I've looked at the Academy Awards with a jaundiced eye.

On another occasion, we were in her living room watching a documentary about the Academy Awards hosted by Patrick Steward. There was a clip in which Louise Tracy accepts an award for her husband, Spencer Tracy. Loretta was fascinated; she had never seen or met Louise Tracy. By the time we were watching this, I knew the story of Loretta and Spencer. He was married but separated when they met on the set of MAN'S CASTLE (1933). Loretta fell madly in love and they had a relationship for a little over a year. Eventually, Loretta broke it off; they were both Catholics and could never marry because he was already married in the church. Clark Gable was the rebound for Loretta. Years later, after Loretta married Tom Lewis, she wrote Spencer a note asking him to stop sending her flowers. Later that year, Tracy met Katharine Hepburn on the set of WOMAN OF THE YEAR.

In 1992, Katharine Hepburn made a TV movie titled THE MAN UPSTAIRS. Ryan O'Neal co-starred as an escaped convict hiding out in her house, and the story was about the relationship that ensued. Loretta experienced a real life situation eerily similar two years earlier. A burglar had come upon her as she was sitting at her sewing table in her bedroom suite. She handwrote an account of what happened and we both saw a seed for a movie script. I wrote a treatment titled "The Burglar" and submitted it to The William Morris Agency. Nothing developed. When the Hepburn movie aired, Loretta opined, "They stole our idea." I shrugged it off. How could you ever prove their idea had been yours?

Here is Loretta's handwritten account which she had handed me the day after the burglar's visit. My name was written on the outside.

Wed. November 14th, 7:00 at night.

I had gone upstairs about 5:00 (p.m.)to walk on the treadmill and then listen to the news.
I had turned off the lights downstairs and turned on the alarm. About 6:30 I went to my bedroom, turned on the T.V. for news, etc.

I had two dresses to shorten –I had not bothered to put on a robe - so I was sitting at my round table pinning a hem – in my bra and panty hose.
I had not heard a sound – no hearing aids in-
All of a sudden I saw a man's feet (in sneakers). Then I saw him: gray jeans, a tan windbreaker and a ski mask. As I looked up, I think I said, "Oh, no!"
He quietly put his hand over my mouth and said, "Don't scream! Don't scream! I'm not going to hurt you." I nodded my head.
"Are you alone?" I said, "Yes."
He repeated, "I'm not going to hurt you. I want your jewelry."
I said, "It's right there in the Lucite box."
He looked in the box and then said, "I want your real jewelry."
I told him, "That's it. You guys have been here before."
He said, "No, I haven't."
I said, "I mean I've been robbed twice before. I could not afford to replace my jewelry so I went to Ceros.
In the meantime, he put 3 or 4 rings he got from the Lucite box into his pocket.
I started to cry and kept repeating that that was it.
 Again he said, "These aren't real."
I said, "No. I paid $700 for that one at Ceros."
He kept saying, "Please don't cry – I'm not going to hurt you," but I couldn't stop even though I was talking all through it. He finally said, "Where's your husband?"
I said, "He's dead."
I kept wondering how he got by the alarm, or maybe he knew how to turn it off – but I was afraid to mention it. Anyway, he said, "I'm sorry. I really don't want to do this but I got a family to

take care of – I have medical expenses and no one ---- *no one* will give me a job of any kind.

I believed him. I felt sorry for him because he had, by this time, put the rings back down on the table and said, "These won't help." I told him I had twenty dollars I could give him and he said, "No, that wouldn't help either."

I went to my wallet in the bag which hung on the door knob and I had $25.00 which I put in his hand – and I told him, "It's better than nothing."

When he first went to the jewel box, I asked if I could put on a robe. He didn't even look at me and said, "Yes." So I went into the bathroom to get a robe; I didn't notice anything; I was too scared.

But, all the time he kept saying, "I'm sorry I frightened you; please stop crying. I don't want to give you a heart attack. I thought no one was here. When I saw you, I was surprised ---I thought the house was empty." The lights were out downstairs. Then I said, "I want to help you some way. I know, I could write you a check for $1000 for cash. Then anyone could endorse it. I promise I won't trace it or you in any way."

He said, "Oh, no. I couldn't do that." The more I urged him the more he said no.

Finally, he said, "Why isn't this property protected by alarms?"

I said, "It is."

He said, "Not in the windows. "I'll show you" – and he did.

He'd come up the trellis outside the dining room and came in the bathroom window.

The night before I was dressing and it would have been worse – my jewelry was all out and ready to wear.

I must say by now he had been so considerate of me, I felt compelled to help him. So, I offered to let him out the front door – he said he'd rather go out the way he came in. I asked him to put my screen back but he said it was bent and that he couldn't and then he asked if I would please turn off the light so he wouldn't be seen climbing down. I did.

He said, "Please, have these windows alarmed. Burglars use windows to get in."

I told him I was glad he hadn't come up the stairs because it would have alarmed and the police would have been here by now.

He said as he left, "Now, don't call the police." I promised – actually, it never dawned on me to call them –the man hadn't hurt me-or taken anything from me and I kept thinking about his own family situation. Oh, he did say, "You have a lot of clothes." I asked what size his wife was. He said, "She's left me. Now, it's just me and the kids."

Also, he said, "This is such a big house. Why don't you have jewelry – or a maid – or someone?"

I said, "Well, it looks big to you –but I bought this house for $150,000 twenty-one years ago and I pay a $700 loan – I can't rent anything for $700 today." He agreed.

I repeated, "I wish there was some way I could help you – I really do."

As he was leaving, I said," I want you to do me a favor. Will you please say," and before I could get it out, he said, "Say a prayer for you." And I said, "Yes, and I'll offer my mass for you tomorrow," which I did.

He climbed out the window, as big as he was, about 190 to 200 lbs., all muscle and tall. He tipped one of my hair spray cans. That was all.

I said, "Be careful."

He said, "Don't worry, this is easy – don't forget to have the alarms put on" – and he was gone.

I shut and locked the windows on the north side of the house --- and went back to my sewing table – but I couldn't concentrate – I looked at the clock; it was 7:18

I hope my sense of security hasn't been demolished. I'd hate to turn into a scaredy cat at my age. I've decided not to tell any of my sisters, they'd just worry – nor Jean – he'll worry. Ed, yes – he has common sense and he can make use of my experience in the book. I don't know what kind of alarms to put on the windows though – I'll have to think long and carefully.

I couldn't help but wonder where the poor man went after he left me – what house did he choose? Did he get enough? Finally, at twelve o'clock last night, I took a sleeping pill and went to sleep.

I hope he's not in trouble. I'll keep praying for him. He really was a good man. All his reactions were kind. He kept saying, "God knows I don't want to do this but I have to get help somewhere – again, I believed him and I hope he didn't get caught. I know that's crazy but I do.

As Loretta implied, she did have the kind of "real jewelry" the man was after, but she kept it in a hidden safe underneath the stairway to the third floor. As much as she felt sorry for the man, she wasn't willing to turn any of those pieces over. I was very familiar with Loretta's good jewelry, as she wore it on occasions for which I was her escort. I also carried her diamonds and emeralds in the inside pocket of my sport's jacket when we travelled. No one would be looking for it on me, and these were days prior to airport security checks.

I had dinner with Loretta and Sally a few evenings after the break-in. Sally now knew about the burglar, and she complained to me how secretive Loretta could be; that seemed to bother her the most. I observed to Loretta one time that she and Sally took turns walking on eggshells around each other. She thought it was an apt description of that particular family dynamic.

Loretta was very gracious to my family. They were excited about my book opportunity and several had met Loretta while visiting California. Loretta hosted me, my sister, Carolyn, and her two children for dinner at an old-time Los Angeles Mexican restaurant. On our way back to Long Beach, Carolyn made the observation that Loretta either didn't wear makeup or she put it on "very, very, carefully." The next day as I was working with Loretta, I quoted Carolyn. Loretta responded, "Tell her I put it on "very, very, carefully." She then explained that she didn't apply a foundation but applied the make-up only to the spots on her face that needed it.

Another sister, Mary Margaret, who is actually a religious Sister, and her good friend, Sister Mary Sue Frieberger, were invited to Loretta's home for dinner, only to be chastised by the hostess for not wearing religious habits. Jean Louis took Mary Margaret aside and whispered, "You look just fine as you are."

I accompanied Loretta on a trip to Chicago and my cousin's son, Jason, stopped by at the Drake Hotel to visit. Jason had called from the lobby before coming up, and I opened the door to the suite so it would be easy for him to find. In the interim I noticed a man, probably in his fifties, take a quick look in and then proceed down the hall. A few minutes after Jason arrived, a bellman knocked on the door with a note for Loretta. It was from the man down the hall and he wanted to hook up with Loretta. She was incensed. "How dare he!" and "Who does he think he is!" and so forth. She wanted to call the desk and complain about the bellman delivering such a note. I talked her out of that. He seemed like a hapless kind of guy, frumpish in appearance and probably easily intimidated.

Jason and I talked about it later that night. Loretta was in her late seventies and guys were still hitting on her. Loretta had been equally impressed with Jason. After he left, she gasped, "He's more handsome than Tyrone (Power)!"

The next day my oldest sister Evelyn hosted Loretta for tea at her condominium. When we entered their door, Evelyn and husband Sidney Friedman were there to greet us. I noticed that Evelyn's hair was wet. I found out later that, between the time we were spotted getting out of the car and reaching their door, Evelyn had jumped in and out of the shower and dressed. She was running behind schedule because of a last moment decision to purchase new dishes. A postscript to this story: once Loretta and I returned to Los Angeles, I realized that she had packed a dress specifically for Evelyn's tea. Loretta always plotted her wardrobe selections strategically, and that she included something special to meet more of my family struck me as very sweet.

Chapter Eight: Loretta Wows Them at the Waldorf

The most impressive occasion at which I was Loretta's escort was to a fundraiser for the Museum of Radio and Television at the Waldorf Astoria in New York City, April 1991. This was the same cause for which Loretta had made the appearance in Los Angeles when I saw her for the first time. Loretta was going to introduce a segment of the program. She had to be coaxed into participating but after she agreed, I understood why the coaxing was necessary. Loretta never did anything halfway, and she worked very hard preparing for the event. Her remarks were written by a speech writer her publicist had engaged. She then tore that apart and put it back together in an effort to make it sound like it came from her lips. Next she wrote it on cue cards that she went over and over until she had it memorized.

What to wear was taken as seriously. Finally, Loretta decided on a floor length gown by Jimmy Galanos that utilized a shiny fabric interspersed with swirls of gold, blue and silver. She then had Jean design a steel blue satin cape, just in case the venue was cool. Packing was an extraordinary effort. Loretta had huge suitcases in which each outfit was wrapped in tissue so that they were "given room to breathe."

From the moment we left her home, this was to be a thorough "Loretta Young" outing. Greg Fischer, a man a few years younger than myself, had started working for Loretta while in high school and, in conjunction with more significant career ventures, continued helping her into the '90s. Driving the Rolls, Greg chauffeured us to Los Angeles International Airport. We flew on MGM, an upscale shuttle to New York that catered to the rich and famous. In fact, on that day they inaugurated menus by Wolfgang Puck who was there in person to welcome us. The seating arrangement was very intimate; our two-seat area had its own entertainment center and each seating area was surrounded by ample space. It was while we were flying from one coast to the other that Loretta told me, "The only reason I'm doing this is for you. I know you like novel experiences and believe me, you're about to have one." I smiled and said thank you, but, in truth, it made me feel uncomfortable because it harkened back to what Sally had said over a year earlier, "Don't you know? This is all for you."

We stayed at the Plaza Anthenee, a luxurious hotel, located on 64th Street, between Park and Madison Avenues. Loretta had a grand suite on the top floor. I was relegated to more modest quarters several floors below. We arrived in plenty of time to reach our hotel and prepare for the big occasion that same evening. Of course I could dress in minutes and did. Loretta, on the other hand, was having a "queen-of-the-silver-screen" fit. It seemed that she didn't like the arrangement of the mirrors in her bathroom. She called and they brought other mirrors with extension arms, but, this effort, too, was unsatisfactory. For a reason I don't recall, I was in her suite when they brought the extending mirrors.

After they left, she said curtly, "They just don't know how to deal with someone like me." My first thought was, "Who would?" Then I took note of the fact that Loretta had traded on her looks for sixty plus years, and by that time she knew better than anyone else what worked for her.

I realized how true that was a short time later while we were riding up the elevator at the Waldorf to the ballroom. I observed Kitty Carlisle and Tony Randall scrutinizing Loretta inches from her face. Were they wondering if she had face-work done or were they amazed that she had maintained her legendary beauty, I'll never know. One thing for sure, Loretta had their attention.

Before entering the ballroom there was another large room where the press was lying in wait. Loretta clutched my arm tightly, and we moved from one media outlet to the next, the initial one's being the print media. Photographers encircled us and snapped away. Eventually I became very familiar with the chant, "Loretta, alone! Loretta, alone!" meaning get the unknown man at her side out of the picture. I would have complied, but Loretta grabbed my arm all the tighter.

Mary Tyler Moore was moving through the room at the same pace right behind us, and Loretta took a moment to introduce me. A few minutes later we caught up with Douglas Fairbanks, Jr., and the photographers went nuts getting pictures of Loretta and Fairbanks together. They must have known that the two had made a number of films together. I was introduced to Fairbanks and told him that I was aware that they had co-starred in six films. He replied, "Six! Were any of them any good?" I responded that I had enjoyed THE LIFE OF JIMMY DOLAN and Fairbanks concurred, "Yes, I think that that one was good."

The electronic media was on the other side of the room, and they were able to question Loretta without me being her shadow. As we were finally leaving the room, I was relieved. The loud and aggressive behavior of the media had been an assault. Maybe I was still fragile from my breakdown but I found it jarring. There was a kind moment, though, right before we left the room. Mary Tyler Moore came to my side and said, "Ed, it was a pleasure to meet you." "Wow," I thought, "she didn't need to do that."

Loretta and I were both at the same table for eight. She was seated between Randolph Hearst, Jr. and Walter Cronkite; I was seated between their wives. Randolph Hearst was the father of Patty Hearst and Veronica Hearst was his Dutch-born, third wife. Mrs. Hearst was quite lovely. I told her that she reminded me of Audrey Hepburn. She said, "Do you think so?" Then with her eyes turning toward Loretta, said, "Most often I hear that I remind people of Loretta Young." Mrs. Hearst, probably younger than I, was an engaging dinner partner. She mentioned that she had previously been married. I don't remember to whom or if it had been more than once, but she had lived both in South America and Monte Carlo. I asked her why the Randolph Hearsts would bother to dress and come out for an occasion such as this on a Thursday night. She replied, "Randy's the only one in his family who works. This is work." I saw what she meant a few minutes later when Katherine Graham, Publisher of *The Washington Post* got up from the next table and headed in the direction of our table. Mrs. Hearst signaled to her husband, and he got up just at the moment she was passing, creating an "accidental" moment in which they exchanged a few words.

Another thing Veronica Hearst said struck me as insightful, "Our friends really aren't very nice people. They have so much money that they don't have to play by the same rules as everyone else, and they don't." I found her totally fascinating, but after a while she said, "You'd better pay attention to Mrs. Cronkite. I think she's getting jealous."

The Betsy Cronkite I encountered that evening was in a cranky mood. She told me about a book her daughter had written about depression. Mrs. Cronkite's attitude was, "Pull yourself up by your bootstraps. None of this babying stuff." I felt that I had an inside track on understanding depression, and it was my judgment that Mrs. Cronkite didn't have a rudimentary clue. I also concluded that if her daughter hadn't been able to elucidate her, I sure wasn't going to wade into those waters.

Also at our table was Abba Eban. I knew that he had been an Ambassador to the United Nations from Israel, but I was more aware of him from the 1984 PBS series, "Heritage, Civilization of the Jews." There was a moment when Mrs. Hearst had left the table, and after violinist, Isaac Stern, who had been standing and visiting with Eban, departed. I spoke across that empty gap, making an effort to introduce myself. I don't recall that he said anything but can vividly remember a gruff look, telegraphing, "Don't bother me."

Loretta was letter perfect in her presentation and appeared to be well-received. However, I heard a slight slurring with words that began with "s." It reminded me of watching her much acclaimed

1986 TV movie, CHRISTMAS EVE, which she made 26 years after leaving series television. I had caught that same slight slurring with "s" words then and wondered if false teeth might be responsible. That night in New York, I knew that she didn't wear false teeth and concluded that it must have been a reaction to stress. I was only half right. I discovered later that she had fallen by her reflecting pool years earlier, knocking out a front tooth. A dentist was able to reinsert it but the slurring with "s" words now became evident whenever she was under stress.

As we were leaving the ballroom, a producer from ABC's GOOD MORNING AMERICA approached Loretta and asked her if she'd be interested in serving as a guest host for the program. "Oh, no, Dear, I'm never up at that hour," Loretta replied glibly. Then Robert Osborne, host of the Turner Classic Movie Channel, approached Loretta to tell her how much he had always admired her. Loretta thanked him but never broke stride. When we reached the ground level and were walking to the street, a photographer asked Loretta to stop so that he could take her picture. She responded, "You'll have to get it on the run," and I suspected she had uttered that sentence countless times over the years.

After being delivered to the hotel by limousine, Loretta asked me to come up to her suite for a nightcap as she needed to unwind. I went to my room to change and gave her a few more minutes to get out of her evening clothes before heading up. After a few minutes, the conversation returned to her telling me that she had agreed to participate in this evening because she thought that I'd enjoy it. I told her that I had and thanked her. Then she asked me about my love life. Had there ever been a serious relationship? I told her that there had but that it had ended badly. She asked me when this had happened and I said, "I really don't like talking about it." It was an abrupt answer but it put an end to a situation which was very uncomfortable for me. Loretta didn't seem offended. Rather, she displayed a "that's/that" attitude and the subject changed.

The discussion, or I should say, non-discussion about my love life was a turning point in my relationship with Loretta. I think from that point on she knew or suspected I was gay. Whenever the subject of homosexuality came up, I always argued that it wasn't a choice and that even Catholic Church teachings concurred. Loretta wasn't buying it. By this time, I knew her opinion well. She had previously stated: "Homosexuality is when someone becomes bored and wants something kinkier." I didn't have the courage to out myself; I was afraid that it would jeopardize the opportunity to write our book. Instead, without words being spoken, I think that Loretta and I instituted the "Don't ask, Don't Tell" policy that President Clinton would introduce a year later. I don't think speechless communication was anything new to Loretta. My impression was that the unspoken had been her mother's modus operandi, and I think Loretta chose that same avenue over confrontation.

The next morning, my brother Kevin, his wife Laura, and their two oldest daughters arrived from their home in Weston, Connecticut. I can still see little Katie, with Loretta's encouragement, running throughout her suite wearing the blue satin cape that Jean Louis had designed for the previous evening's event.

Later, Loretta and I went to Mass at St. Patrick's during which a fan pushed her way into our pew to chat with Loretta. After that, we joined a gentleman from the Museum of Radio and Television for Lunch at "21." As we walked in, Loretta greeted the maitre'd, saying, "Hello, Paul." He must have been there for a long time; it had been the late '60s since Loretta maintained an apartment in New York. That night we were the guests of a real estate magnate whose name I don't remember. He invited us to join his party at Le Circ. We were at a large table, and Loretta was out of ear shot from where I was sitting. I was glad. The two women on each side of me were having a conversation about Leona Helmsley and how she had snagged Harry Helmsley away from his former wife by giving him blowjobs under the desk. Loretta once opined that I was a bigger prude than she; she may have been right.

A year to the month later, Loretta and I shared a very different event. The Rodney King Riots were a response to a jury acquittal of four white policemen in the videotaped beating of Rodney King, a black man. The riots lasted six days and cost a billion dollars in damage. The first night of the mayhem, I received a phone call from Loretta's son Peter. He had called his mother and begged her to leave Beverly Hills and come to his home in Solvang. She refused. Peter then called me to ask if I'd drive into Beverly Hills and spend the night. I tried to convince him that the riots would never cross Wilshire Boulevard and that his mother was in no danger. He persisted so I agreed to go in. What ordinarily would take 50 minutes at that time of night took close to four hours. It seemed like I was in a disaster movie. Tens of thousands of people fleeing Los Angeles created such gridlock that I felt I was moving only inches at a time. Finally I arrived and Loretta answered the door. She knew I was coming, and we watched the news coverage into the early morning hours.

The next morning, I talked to Peter and he now agreed that the danger had passed. I was determined to get back to Long Beach even though there was a curfew. Whereas the night before, the 405 Freeway was at a standstill, now it was eerily deserted. I don't remember seeing any vehicles other than military, but for some reason, no one stopped me in my attempt to return to my apartment. At one point I was right behind a mounted tank, much like one I knew in Vietnam. It was manned with soldiers, aiming machine guns in all directions. When I looked to the east, there was one community after another either still in flames or smoldering smoke. This continued all the way until I exited onto the Long Beach Freeway. Long Beach had not been spared. I would learn later that there were two hundred fires in that city alone. When I finally arrived at my neighborhood, I parked in my usual spot a half block away on a very expensive street of single family homes. The sky was blue, the yards well-manicured, the birds chirping. I couldn't help but be aware of societal inequities.

Loretta with sons Peter (left) and Chris (right) 1n 1976. I would meet them three years later

Loretta's last Beverly Hills home. She purchased it from Sydney Guilaroff, MGM's famous hairdresser. Gladys would need a year and a half to fine-tune it for her movie star daughter.

Loretta in her Rolls, departing for Saturday night mass at The Church of the Good Shepherd in Beverly Hills.

Jean Louis and Maggie Fisher depart for their honeymoon in 1955. For the next thirty-four years, they would be among Loretta's closest friends.

Loretta's close friend from childhood, Jane Mullen Sharpe. She was Jane Del Amo when this picture was taken in the '40s.

Loretta and Me. Loretta gave me this picture for Christmas, 1990.

Me photographed with Loretta's Oscar. I wouldn't have been such a fruitcake had Loretta been in the room. Note the portrait on the wall. It is the one described by Loretta in *Behind the Door: the Real Life of Loretta Young* as capturing the fragility of her life at that time.

Loretta with my sister Evelyn and husband Sidney Friedman in Chicago. Evelyn hosted a tea in Loretta's honor. Loretta packed that outfit specifically to wear for Evelyn's tea. I thought that was very sweet of her.

Chris and Linda often accompanied Loretta on formal occasions. They were networking for their own production company, The Entertainment Group.

Loretta's 80th birthday party at Jimmy's in Beverly Hills. Left to right: Jim (Polly Ann's son) and Eva Hermann, Chris and Linda Lewis, Loretta, Jack Lindley (Loretta's brother), Sally Foster, Caesar Romero, Polly Ann Hermann, Georgiana Montalban.

Jean and Loretta in their Palm Springs living room. Loretta made the kaftan she is wearing; she made many others for friends. Also, note that Loretta has kicked her shoes off, not to look taller than Jean.

Loretta in Palm Springs. No air-brushing; this is how she really looked in her mid-eighties.

Salvador Iglesias, Loretta's biggest collector, Jean and Loretta, standing in front of the Palm Springs home.

Chapter Nine: The Why of Loretta's Marriage to Jean Louis

I willingly allowed Loretta's world to eclipse my own. The only gay things going on were hanging out with a few friends and attending monthly meetings of Communidad, a gay gathering at St. Matthew's parish in Long Beach. I believe that it was the first of its kind. Most parishes had traditionally organized men's groups and women's groups. St. Matthew's went a step further and formed one for gays and lesbians. I thought it amusing that, among all the groups, we had the best turnout for fundraising breakfasts because of the culinary creativity of gay men. Cardinal Mahoney came to visit us a couple times. Once he said Mass, and another time he attended a pitch-in dinner.

I had met Cardinal Mahoney at a function with Loretta prior to being re-introduced to him at St. Mathews. Surprisingly, he said, "I know, Ed Funk." The real surprise, however, would have been Loretta's, had she learned that the Cardinal was lending support to a gay parish association in Long Beach.

As it turned out Loretta had other matters on her mind that would prove life-changing. Before Maggie Louis died, she asked Loretta to assume responsibility as Jean's financial conservator. Maggie had viewed Jean as a creative genius but realized early in their marriage that he had no head for business; she subsequently assumed those responsibilities. Her concern was that after her death, some woman would view Jean as ripe-for-the-pickings and take advantage of him financially.

For the first two years after Maggie's death, Jean managed well on his own, scooting between Montecito and Paris. Then senility seemed to set in quickly. He traveled to New York to attend an award presentation and, after checking into his hotel, forgot why he was there and failed to attend the show. Ricardo and Georgiana attended the affair and, concerned about Jean's no-show, checked on him later that night.

Back in Montecito, one of Jean's neighbor's, a French woman who had married five times, took an interest in Jean. However, after keeping an eye on him for a couple of months, she tired of the mission and decided that he needed to be placed in an assisted living facility. She wasn't after his money; she had plenty of her own. But she did decide that Jean's will needed to be changed so that the designee would be one of her favorite charities. Upon learning of Loretta's financial involvement in Jean's affairs, the French woman's lawyer sent Loretta a form to sign, surrendering her role as financial conservator.

With her own lawyer in tow, Loretta met with the opposing attorney in Montecito and said, "This is exactly the kind of thing that Maggie feared. You put Jean in a home and he won't last two months." She refused to cooperate. Her stand was admirable, but here she was at age 79 responsible for an 83-year-old man who was slipping into senility. Loretta brought Jean to her home. Jean was happy to leave Montecito, too many memories of Maggie.

Loretta's son Chris and daughter-in-law Linda traveled with their work and Loretta decided to use their home in Palm Springs, thinking that the desert sun would be good for Jean. After spending several weeks and seeing Jean's positive response, Loretta decided that they should buy a home there. For one thing, it would provide a solution of what to do with Jean's furniture, products of Gladys Belzer's decorating.

After six months of keeping her books, his books, and their books, Loretta decided that they should marry to simplify their arrangement. I was visiting with Loretta in her Beverly Hills kitchen the night before their quiet wedding was to occur, and Jean Louis shuffled in and asked, "Now, what day are we getting married?" Loretta replied, "Tomorrow, dear," and then looked at me as if to say, "Look what I'm getting myself into." I thought to myself, "This time around, it's not all about you."

It wasn't the first time I had witnessed Loretta "getting out of herself." Her other "best friend" in addition to Josie Wayne, was Jane Sharpe. Loretta and Jane had known each other since boarding school days; Gladys had sent the girls off for a couple of years when she married George Belzer. They attended two different schools, both in the Los Angeles area. Ramona was the second and attracted the daughters of well-to-do parents (The nuns made an exception in Gladys's case and allowed her to pay tuition on an installment basis). Loretta and Jane soon celebrated their tenth birthdays together and a friendship took hold that lasted the next seventy years.

I met Jane and her husband, Dr. John Sharpe, shortly after meeting Loretta. They were both seriously ill with cancer. Even with their health challenges, they were stimulating company, and I often chauffeured them from their Palos Verdes home to Loretta's. The occasion was usually Mass at Loretta's home (she had no end of priest friends willing to oblige) followed by a luncheon.

John had been the Chief of Staff at St. John's Hospital in Santa Monica and, prior to that, had been Ronald Reagan's physician. The day before John died, the former President called and spoke with him for forty-five minutes. This information surprised me. Much had been written about Reagan's resistance to intimate relationships outside of his bond with Mrs. Reagan, yet visiting with someone on their deathbed is inherently intimate.

During the last year of Jane's life, Loretta spent her weekends at Jane's home caring for her and allowing a break for Jane's daughter, Hillary. Jane had said, "Oh, Honey, I'm afraid you'll get so bored coming down here." Loretta responded, "Jane, at this point in our lives, you are my plan, my project, *you*! So don't you worry about my being bored." Both women had spent most of their lives living in lavish homes. Now, Jane's world was reduced to one bedroom with a view of a quiet street, heavily shaded by massive eucalyptus trees. It would be within this quiet room that the friendship between these two woman would achieve its deepest intimacy.

It was only a few months after Jane died that Loretta assumed responsibility for Jean, and within a year they had purchased their Palm Springs residence. This home looked like something where the Jetsons, the animated sitcom family from the '60s, might have lived. A single story structure, the exterior looked like a white stucco space ship. The main interior feature was a huge circular living room, off of which there was a formal dining alcove and another alcove that served as a den. A crescent-shaped swimming pool circled outside the rear. Loretta eventually enclosed the patio space between the pool and living room with a curved Plexiglas interval, the addition's circular line now following the curved line of the pool. There was a service wing with kitchen and servant's quarters and a bedroom wing with two bedroom suites. Loretta assumed the larger suite and decided to have the shower removed to be replaced with her makeup station. Her rationale was, "I don't take showers." A thought I kept to myself : "You're eighty-years old! You're not going to live forever, and the next people to buy this house will want a shower." But it was her house.

The Palm Springs home presented a challenge. Her mother had always assumed decorating responsibility in every home Loretta had lived. All Loretta had to do was move in. One afternoon, Loretta was in an anxious mood regarding some decorating decisions and she recognized that she was becoming irritable. She said to me, "I hope I don't boot this thing." I knew what she meant. She saw this opportunity for taking care of Jean as God-sent and she didn't want to blow it by being cross.

Loretta was having trouble finding a fabric to recover Jean's Lucite chairs which would be arranged by the fireplace in the living room. She had consulted upholsterers with no luck. Finally one day I was in the car with Loretta and Jean, and she was lamenting her lack of success finding the fabric. Jean pointed to a Jo Ann's Fabric store and told her to pull in. We weren't in the store five minutes when Jean selected a fabric that satisfied Loretta. But, amazingly, it was the intended underside of the fabric he chose! Jean hadn't lost his touch.

I learned about designing clothes, mainly from Loretta's explaining to me how Jean had approached his work. For a film he would begin by reading the script to understand the mood of the scene. Then he'd review a large selection of fabrics. When he found one he liked, the way it felt and draped in his hand propelled the sketch of the design. I would have thought that the design came first.

Jean was a soft-spoken gentle soul who never had a bad word to say about anyone. I tried any number of times to get him to gossip about the famous women he dressed, and the only time he took the bait was when Katharine Hepburn's name came up. She provoked him by dictating what he should design and how. She had no interest in hearing his ideas.

Loretta also seldom had negative things to say about other actresses. There were only a few exceptions. I asked her why Jane Wyman always wore a hairdo with bangs. Loretta's response: "The poor dear. What else can she do with that forehead?" The other comment was about Celeste Holm who co-starred with Loretta in the 1949 film, COME TO THE STABLE. Loretta recalled that Celeste had told her that it was her intention to be a leading lady, not stay relegated to the second lead. Loretta thought to herself, "It will never happen, Dear, you don't have a chin."

I wasn't too surprised that Loretta didn't have a glowing impression of Joan Crawford; they got off to a bad start when Loretta was only fourteen and Joan saw her as unwanted competition. However, Sally and Joan remained life-long friends, and Loretta related a story Sally had told her when she went to see Joan's adopted son, Christopher, for the first time. Joan took Sally to the nursery and toddler Christopher's arms were strapped to the sides of the crib. Sally exclaimed, "Joan, you can't do that to a child" to which Joan replied, "There will be no masturbation in this house!"

Loretta also was not an admirer of Marlene Dietrich. One day, while riding in the car with Loretta and Jean, Loretta explained how Jean's ingenious designs for Marlene Dietrich were central to her late career as a concert artist. It wasn't her singing that drew the crowds, but the fact that she still looked so glamorous at an advanced age. She wore a perfectly coiffed blonde wig and utilized masterful lighting, but it was Jean Louis' conjuring that created the real magic. She wore a gold lame gown, form fitted to show off her curves, accompanied with a white fox fur. In reality she no longer had these curves; she was a skinny, elderly woman. Jean created the gown by shaping her *pretend* body with chicken wire and smooth foam and then covering it with the gold lame fabric. All Dietrich had to do was to step into it and be zipped up. Jean was not pleased that Loretta was divulging his trade secrets to me, but she couldn't be contained.

Loretta did share some interesting stories about her interactions with four other famous stars, Elizabeth Taylor, Rita Hayworth, Betty Grable, and Lorraine Day.

There were actually three anecdotes related to Elizabeth Taylor. The first involved a very young Elizabeth when she was engaged to Nicky Hilton, who would become her first husband. Hilton was Catholic and Elizabeth was not. Cardinal McIntyre of Los Angeles called Loretta and asked if she would invite Elizabeth to her home and explain the Catholic teachings on birth control. Loretta remembered watching Elizabeth driving up to the house in a yellow Cadillac convertible, noticing how stunningly beautiful she was. As they sat down to talk, Elizabeth uttered in exasperation, "I know we're supposed to talk about birth control, but what do those old men know!" Loretta, sizing up her assignment as futile, replied, "Honey, let's just have lunch!"

The second story involved a party in the '80s. Shortly after arriving, Loretta eyed piles of what looked like cocaine on separate flat mirrors. Elizabeth came up behind her and said, "Loretta, dear, get out of here. This isn't your kind of party." Loretta turned to Elizabeth and said, "I think you're right," found her escort and left. She appreciated Elizabeth's protective concern for her.

The last Elizabeth Taylor anecdote took place when Loretta entered a Beverly Hills restaurant with her hosts, a couple not associated with the movie industry. Spotting Elizabeth, the wife was very much star struck, and Loretta offered to introduce the couple to her. Elizabeth had just come from a very successful

AIDS fundraiser and was celebrating with friends. Loretta made the introduction and Elizabeth was quite gracious. While the couple was momentarily distracted, Elizabeth gave Loretta a knowing wink, indicating her understanding that they were both being kind to Loretta's "civilian" friends.

The Rita Hayworth encounter occurred at Samuel Goldwyn Studios where Loretta was filming her television show and Rita was making a film; Loretta thought later that it may have been SEPARATE TABLES. The two women met in a hallway and Loretta noticed that there were tears in Rita's eyes. She asked, "Rita, honey, what's wrong?" Rita replied, "That's just it, Loretta. I don't know. But something's wrong." Loretta assured her that she'd pray for her and ask her mother to pray for her as well. Years later, when Rita's Alzheimer's diagnosis became known, Loretta thought back to that interchange in the hallway.

The Betty Grable moment came when she and Loretta were making films concurrently at 20th Century-Fox. Loretta had wandered onto a soundstage where Betty was working, as stars apparently were allowed to do. Betty was doing a musical number and her maid was standing off camera. When Betty had a break, she came over and grabbed a glass of orange juice off the tray. Loretta walked up to Betty and, as they were chatting, she grabbed the glass of juice that had been returned to the tray and took a gulp. It contained more vodka than juice and Loretta exclaimed, "How can you drink this and dance so exquisitely?" Betty replied, "How do you think I can be dancing this early in the morning?"

The Lorraine Day encounter took place when both were attending a White House luncheon during World War II. Mrs. Roosevelt had pointed the way to a powder room for Loretta and Lorraine. As they returned to the dining room, Lorraine said to Loretta, "Just this once, I'd love to see you fall flat on that pretty face of yours!" Loretta was stunned and clueless as to the provocation.

Another anecdote concerned Frank Sinatra although it relates to Loretta's mother rather than herself. Gladys owned an apartment house on Wilshire in the '50s and one of her tenants was Sinatra. This was after Ava Gardner had left him, and Gladys told her daughters that as she passed his apartment in the hall, she could hear him listening to the love songs of his own records. Certainly a unique way of dealing with his grief.

Chapter Ten: Estrangement with Daughter Judy

Delores Hope had been a big band singer in her youth, and in her eighties, went into a studio and recorded an album for her friends. When Loretta and I were driving around Palm Springs, we often listened to Delores's tape. Her voice was surprisingly smooth, but I was quite aware that no one else in their cars was listening to Delores Hope!

Riding with Loretta at the wheel became more of an adventure as the years passed. Her most egregious error was running red lights. I called this to her attention, but her reaction was, "Here in the desert, it really doesn't matter." She was right to the degree that the risks were less than in Los Angeles. Which brings me to her sister's driving. Sally had a lead foot. One day I was riding with her on a quiet residential street in Beverly Hills and she actually passed a car. Sensing that I was taken back, she uttered, "Can't they see that I'm trying to maintain a certain momentum!"

There was certainly no momentum in Loretta's relationship with her daughter Judy. They were estranged when I entered Loretta's life and continued to be so. I didn't realize how upsetting this was to Loretta until one night at the Bistro (restaurant) in Beverly Hills. We were walking toward our table, and Loretta stopped for a moment and said, "Judy?" Apparently, she thought that the woman was her daughter. She didn't respond and we continued on. I hadn't met Judy yet, but I had seen pictures and couldn't figure out how Loretta could have been so mistaken. The woman had been blonde and about the same age, but that was the extent of a resemblance. It struck me as very strange.

Loretta had explained the evolution of their estrangement. Judy had been approached by a publisher to write her story of being the love child of Loretta and Clark Gable. According to Loretta, the publisher expected Judy to elicit Loretta's cooperation in providing all the details of Loretta and Clark's relationship and the ensuing drama of a movie star secretly giving birth to a baby.

Loretta adamantly refused to cooperate. Judy was determined to proceed. Greg Fischer had described Judy to be much like her mother: "She has a very calm manner about her. She looks like her mother, only blonde. She's sophisticated with an appreciation for style and dress. But both Judy and her mother have very strong personalities. The acorn does not fall far from the tree." This last shared attribute apparently set the template that eventually led to non-communication between the two.

The following conversation between Loretta and me shed some light regarding Loretta's view of the estrangement with her daughter. I'm surprised I found this snippet in my transcripts because every time Loretta was about to share something very personal, she'd look at my tape recorder and say, "Turn that thing off", or "Turn that damn thing off." Somehow, this survived.

Loretta: I don't have the energy to fight.

Ed: Maybe that's the problem with Judy. She's got this anger and you don't want to confront it.

Loretta: Oh, I haven't got the energy to cope with that anymore.

Ed: What's the worst that would happen?

Loretta: Nothing, except we wouldn't get any place that we're not at right now. It would probably take me a week to get over the saber cuts that she would get in…..

Ed: What I think has angered Judy about you…..she could make the point that "Loretta Young" was more important. The fact that you didn't tell her that you were her own mother ……she'd say, "Wait a minute……we all want to matter……we all want to think we matter in this life and you're saying I don't matter enough to know that you were my own mother…."

Loretta: Well… Yes, I can see this….

Ed: I'm only saying this as an adversary……

Loretta: I find it invalid. That's *her* point of view. My point of view is that it's my life and, I'm sorry. Yes. Self-preservation is that first law of nature. I consider *me* before I consider Judy. Now, right or wrong. That's what I do.

Ed: Why does it have to be one way or the other?

Loretta: Because it always is with people.

Ed: Why would the truth of the situation, just between the two of you, let's say when she was twelve-years-old or something……

Loretta: Because if you can't keep your own secret, don't expect anyone else to. Particularly someone who is involved. I know enough about human nature that in her case, had it been Buddy Hackett, she would not have been so anxious to have the world know. And he (Gable) never recognized her. Now she has to do what she thinks is right for *her* to do. It's diametrically opposed to my wishes, but that won't have any effect on her because she too thinks of Judy first.

Ed: Do you respect her for that?

Loretta: I don't respect her for it. I admit that's the way it will be. No, I don't respect her because her motives are not valid. When you put them against my motives, her motives are purely and utterly selfish. Mine are not. Mine are protective.

Ed: ……protective to you…..

Loretta: Me …… and her, strangely enough, and to her begat……and my mother…… and my family and anybody else who had anything whatever to do with this. I wouldn't want to dis-edify one person ….. whether a stone be tied around my neck……

Ed: Still, people want validation….

Loretta: That's too damn bad if they want validation. People want a lot of things they can't have.

Ed: They want to know they matter.

Loretta: That's not the way to know. If they don't know when you give birth to them that they matter……that I didn't have an abortion……she'll never know.

Ed: But her argument could be, "Well, that wasn't me….. I was just a baby at that point…. But how about the me who grew up and loved you?

Loretta: Ah, ha, until you were fifty-one-years-old, and suddenly I no longer love you. You thought I loved you until I wouldn't pay your tuition to go to a school I didn't approve. You still accept my paying the lion's share of your monthly mortgage. At this point, I really don't love my daughter at all because she is just too cold to me. I really don't. But I would do anything I can to help her if I could.

Another explanation for their estrangement came down to this: Loretta felt that it was her story the publishers were after, one they had no right to. Without her mother's help, Judy was faced with the challenge of telling a story of which she knew very little.

As for the book I was writing, I started out with a couple of big handicaps. One was that Loretta didn't want an autobiography but a biography told mainly in a third person voice, quoting her and everyone else who participated. This presented two problems: it separated the reader from Loretta as the first person story teller as well as creating an awkward structure. In addition, Loretta did not want to talk about Clark Gable/Judy and, of course, this was the story the publishers wanted. Still, I was convinced that whatever I put together would have an eager market; I was quite willing to press on.

I didn't show Loretta any of the book for the first six months. A month after I did, she informed me that she wanted to rewrite the material. I don't remember her explanation but the real reason was this: I was quoting her real voice and she wanted everything to sound like "Loretta Young." Following are two examples of her rewrites:

The first is about a phone call that Loretta had with Louise, Spencer Tracy's wife. Loretta had met a doctor who told her he could bring hearing ability to anyone with hearing loss, and she immediately thought of John Tracy, Spencer and Louise Tracy's son. Loretta didn't want to call Spencer; this was after their relationship ended, and she was afraid he'd misconstrue the intent of her call.

Here's the original version: "I got up the courage to call up Louise Tracy. I told her about the doctor's ideas on hearing loss. I don't know if she went ahead with anything, but at least she was not rude to me. I think she was surprised, but she was certainly polite, and, if not charming, she was not cold either."

Version two: "I called the boy's mother, Louise. When she came to the phone, I told her about this doctor who claimed to have a cure for hearing loss. To my relief, she was not rude - she was polite - thanked me and rang off. I don't know if she ever followed up on the information but I was left with a feeling of respect for this wife and mother who behaved so beautifully under the circumstances."

The second example refers to Loretta giving some advice to co-star Ray Milland while they were filming 1939's THE DOCTOR TAKES A WIFE. Milland, whose real first name was Jack, was concerned about performing a drunk scene. Loretta asked him if he'd ever been drunk himself, thinking he could recall the experience as a reference.

Original version: "He said, 'Yes, but I don't know how I am.' I suggested, 'Well, just laugh all the time; be one of those drunks.' The minute he hit on the happy drunk, his worries were over and he had a ball with it. Years later, Jack did have a marvelous performance in LOST WEEKEND and that was as a serious drunk. That's what he would naturally be because he's Welsh and they're……….well, everything is way down there."

Version two (again, responding to the question, "Have you ever been drunk?"): 'Yes, but I'm inside looking out, I don't know what I do - or look like, even.' Kidding, I suggested he choose one of the happy drunks who just laugh at everything. He grabbed it and he was charming in the finished product - in direct contrast to his Academy Award winning role as an alcoholic in LOST WEEKEND five years later. At any rate, he sent me roses the next day for my 'private coaching' as he called it. I was delighted."

Also, Loretta didn't like anything hanging in the air without resolution. I told her that by addressing everything as it developed, she was getting ahead of the story. It would be like re-writing the script of a movie and ignoring the director's vision of how the film was to unfold. She didn't buy it. She didn't trust my vision. I didn't like it, but I also knew she was calling the shots. We trudged on. I'd write a chapter. She'd rewrite the chapter. I'd incorporate her rewrites.

Loretta took her Catholic faith very seriously and spending time with her also awakened my faith. I began to pray in a more concrete way. I was really hoping that I might meet a good man to be my partner, and one day, while at Mass in Long Beach, it dawned on me to pray for the right guy. This was just before the Rite of Peace, an interlude before Communion at which time you turn and greet your neighbors. When I turned to the person behind me, it was a guy named Mark whom I knew casually from the Communidad parish group for gays and lesbians. I instantly wondered, "Is God answering my prayer so quickly? Is Mark the guy?"

Mark was a handsome, large-framed man with light brown hair and brown eyes. He wore glasses and had a trimmed beard. His face was both kind and sardonic. At six foot two, he was two inches taller than me. A landscape architect by education and trade, he came to Southern California to join friends whom he had met at Louisiana State University. In the interim, he had worked in Houston.

I looked for Mark at the next Communidad and was told he had returned to his hometown in Louisiana. Maybe he'd return; maybe he wouldn't. The answer to my prayer was now on hold. Mark did return six weeks later, having decided to give California another try.

I called and asked if he wanted to see a movie. He said yes, that he was hoping to see USED PEOPLE, a film with Shirley MacLaine and Marcello Mastroianni. I said, "Sure," even though Shirley MacLaine annoyed me. But my personal bias that the actress seemed too needy on the screen took a back seat to the opportunity to spend an afternoon with Mark. More than the movie, I remember walking around the exterior of the strip mall after the film was over, with me doing most of the talking. I was thrilled about my writing project with Loretta and how it all came together at just the right time, and that I didn't think that that was an accident. Rather than scaring Mark off, he seemed impressed with my enthusiasm and self-assurance.

We continued to find reasons to get together almost every day that week. What I couldn't figure out was: were we dating or were we just two guys becoming better friends? Finally, after walking him to his car one night, I leaned in and gave him a kiss on the cheek. As it turned out, he was having the same quandary, hoping we were dating but not sure. Within seconds of that simple kiss, we were dating.

It was wonderful to be seeing someone. I was like a teenager falling head-over-heels for the first time. Mark had a wonderful voice, fairly deep with just a hint of a southern accent. I had a message machine and I remember listening to one of his messages over and over again. As for Mark, he later told me that he fell for me while watching the playful way I added dried cherries to some cream of wheat I was preparing. Who can explain the mysteries of amour? I was sixteen years older than Mark. Upon discussion, we both said it didn't matter.

I was now very happy on two fronts. I continued to have high hopes for the Loretta book, regardless of hurdles, and I was ecstatic with Mark. I decided that this time I would fall in love without reservation.

Chapter Eleven: Judy's Bruising Tell-all Book

My romance with Mark began in the spring of 1993 and we spent the following Christmas with his family in Louisiana. When I returned to California, there was a harsh reality on the horizon. I became concerned that, as Judy's publishing date was nearing, Loretta was predicting that Judy wouldn't go through with it. This was irrationality on a new level. From my understanding, the publisher had paid an advance and the book was written. What could Judy do, even if she wanted? And, there was no reason to believe that she wanted the project halted.

So, when Judy's book *Uncommon Knowledge* was published in 1994, Loretta had set herself up for a major crisis. I read the book. Initially Loretta had no interest or, more aptly, no stomach for reading it. She kept saying, "I can't believe it. The child that I was protecting is the one out there telling everyone about it." I thought she was sincere. But I also knew that it had been herself as well that she had been protecting from scandal for fifty-nine years, a situation that most people no longer saw as scandal, and hadn't for decades.

I persuaded Loretta to read the book. She got a hundred pages into it and became sick to her stomach. She didn't go any further. However, she read far enough to conclude from her perspective that Judy was playing fast and loose with the facts, such as Judy's description of a visit she had with Gable and her mother. Judy described the scenario as her coming home from school one afternoon and finding her mother and Clark Gable in the living room. Her mother disappeared, leaving her the opportunity to visit with Gable for a couple of hours. It was a warm, friendly visit and Gable would cuff Judy's chin and kiss her on the forehead as he said goodbye. That would be the only time they would meet. Lovely story but Loretta denied it ever happened. Loretta said that Gable had come to their home one time for a business meeting regarding the 1950 movie, KEY TO THE CITY, in which they co-starred. Loretta then escorted Gable to their pool where Judy was swimming with her friend, Mary Frances Griffin, Irene Dunne's daughter, along with other girls. They all giggled at meeting "The King."

Loretta now realized that I'd have to address the story of her and Gable in our book. One day, she handed me a note written on the back of a Kodak box lid. It was her suggestion of what the author (me) should write regarding the Judy/Gable saga:

> "I don't think "hurting her career" per se ever entered her mind - I do think (from those who knew her intimately at the time) that adultery, spreading scandal, giving bad example, were very much on her mind – and that's the reason she chose to exercise her right to privacy, to take the position of, "It was a rumor then, it's a rumor now, and it will always be a rumor," period! I know that she has said more than once – my sins are private between God and me. I don't believe in public confession."

This was hardly the salacious material publishers wanted, but it was a fresh step for Loretta to publically acknowledge the truth of the Judy/Gable saga.

One night in Palm Springs, if still unwilling to go into the details of her relationship with Clark Gable, Loretta was open to discussing how the book had affected the relationship between her and Judy. Loretta elaborated on the phone call, years earlier, during which the book was first discussed. "One day Judy called and said, 'I've just been offered $100,000 to write my story.' I asked, 'What story?' She said, 'My story with you and *you know* and it could be so wonderful, so romantic.' I said, 'If you're asking my permission, you don't have it.' We discussed it a little while and I said, 'This was my mistake. We all do things that we're not proud of, some of us do worse things than others. This was mine. I've already gone to confession and been forgiven. Now there's no reason why it should become a public scandal, a public disgrace for everyone connected with it.' At the time, Judy seemed to understand and was sensitive to my feelings on the matter. My position has never changed. As far as the world is concerned, it's none of their business.

"I'm having a hard time reading Judy's book because it breaks my heart. I can't believe the misinterpretations, the misrepresentations, the phony psychology I hear in all the stories that she makes up and then assigns motives to people for what they're doing. She couldn't possibly know what was in other people's minds, particularly when she was five years old. I mean complete fabrication of stories that just never happened. Never happened!

"I don't know why I'm reading this book. I think it's because you have to look at the dead body and see that it's all bloody. And, the point is, it's not the book. The book really can't hurt me. But Judy, she can and she has. She has destroyed my trust in her, and that's what I'm grieving about more than anything.

"I haven't spoken about this as openly with my family because I don't want to hurt them anymore than they have been. When they call, I say, 'I'm fine, don't worry,' but this has probably been the most difficult thing I've ever faced in my entire life."

In all the years I knew her, Loretta was at her most vulnerable that evening. I can still see her, sitting on her desk chair, turned toward me as I sat on the sofa. Jean's dog, Theda, was sitting at her feet, which was strange because Loretta didn't particularly like Theda and Theda didn't like Loretta. It was as if the little terrier sensed Loretta's sadness and was commiserating. Most poignant for me that night was Loretta's declaration that I was her best friend. That was the only time she would say that to me. Even then, I put it in perspective. She had life-long friends such as Josie Wayne and Jane Sharpe, but, for some reason, I was the one with whom she felt comfortable sharing her most intimate feelings.

Even at that, Loretta was unable to open up and let the Gable story flow; I think she still thought that she'd be putting her soul in jeopardy. Instead, she told me, "I have no control over what others might tell you." By this time I knew Loretta well enough to translate this to mean, "You can go to Polly Ann and Sally and get what they know."

I called both Polly Ann and Sally, quoted Loretta, and scheduled interviews. I saw Sally first. While Sally was often high strung, that afternoon she was extraordinarily so. We were sitting at her dining room table, and at one point she picked up some papers I had laid down and threw them at me, saying, "How can you ask me that question?" I wish I remembered the question, but I don't. However I do remember thinking the reaction was far out of proportion. Polly Ann was always more even-tempered and so was our meeting. From these two encounters I would learn much of what I was initially able to write about the Gable/Judy saga in the book.

Their comments:

Sally: "What the hell choice did Loretta have? If she were my child, I would have wanted her, too. But it's been very hard on Loretta, very hard, all the way through. Working so hard to support every one, and putting up with Tom, and trying to smooth the way for Judy. Who would believe that it would be the daughter, the child who Loretta was protecting, that would drag the scandal into the public. And making it sound like her mother had an on-going sexual relationship with a married man. That's not what happened, and she damn well knows it!"

Polly Ann: "My own personal opinion is that something has been working on Judy for a number of years. Judy had not been a successful actress; her marriage did not work out; she was not a prominent person, and I think she wanted all of that, and I think these are reasons why she decided to write the book. It was one way of getting the notoriety. You could tell by watching the television screen when she was running around from show to show, promoting her book. When I watched her, I was curious to know how she would behave. She loved every minute of it. She was very sure of herself, smiling as though she was thinking, 'Now all the people are noticing me and who I am.' I was shocked when she was asked on THE LARRY KING SHOW 'Did your mother ever try reconciliation?' She said, 'No, never.' Well, I know that wasn't true because I saw the note with Loretta's message, 'Let's have lunch, Honey, and talk.' Judy responded that she didn't feel that the time was right but that she'd let her know. How could she deny that ever happened on THE LARRY KING SHOW?"

Sally also shared that Gladys had had a foreshadowing of what was to come shortly before she died at age ninety-six in 1984. Sally recalled, "Mom was staying with Polly Ann, and Judy had been over. Just by the way that Judy was talking and laughing, Mom sensed that something wasn't right. Later, she said to me, 'You know, Dear, I think that Judy's going to cause trouble. Oh, yes, I really think that Judy's going to create a big scandal. She's just too insensitive. Thank heavens I won't be alive.'"

What is one to make of all this? I think most people would conclude that Judy had not been well served in being allowed to think that Loretta was her adopted mother, particularly since she didn't know the truth until she was thirty-one-years-old. Even her aunts and grandmother had pushed for disclosure a decade earlier but were vetoed by Loretta. Reasonable people could have differing opinions on whether Judy's need to tell her story trumped her mother's quest for privacy in what she saw as scandal and the possible fallout from the example it set. What was clear to me was that Loretta, her sisters, and even their mother from the grave, circled the wagons after Judy's book came out. Judy was the bad guy.

I had also called Peter, Loretta's younger son, to see if he could shed some light on the Judy saga. He related a Mother's Day dinner, 1986. Loretta, Judy, Peter, and a family friend were in attendance. Judy was already working on her book and it was a fragile time. Recalls Peter, "I don't remember what happened at the table except that my mom said something to Judy and Judy said something back. I didn't realize what was going on until there was this pregnant pause, then it was like lightning went back and forth and Mom left the table. I really didn't know what it was about, and I don't think they did. But a rule had been broken. Not so much in the last couple of years, but it used to be the rule in Mom's house that you had to keep everything under control. At this point, Judy didn't do it; she didn't play the game.

"My mom went upstairs and I went after her. I followed her into her bathroom and put my arms around her. It was weird; I think it threw her because she was used to being the strong one, not the other way around. Mom was crying. I heard Judy come up the stairs and then she was right behind me. Judy was scary that night. I remember looking out from the bathroom, seeing them both framed by the doorway, nose-to-nose, and it was the first time I've seen my mom on the defensive. It wasn't the kind of encounter I had ever had with her. You can't go after her like an equal; it's not what she did with her mother and that's not what you do with her. But Judy did it. Mom was trying to defend herself. I remember her saying, 'Well, your father didn't want you.' Judy said something like, 'I'm not your mortal sin.' There was a lot of dialogue like that but I don't remember the exact words. The thing went on a little longer. My mother told Judy, 'I was always there for you,' and Judy started railing against her. I said, 'No, that's true, Judy. Don't bend that into anything other than what it is. If someone is there for you, then they are, and Mom has been there for all of us."

"Everything that was said was said in such a flurry of temper-and-feeling that it was like a floodgate had opened. My mom was into damage control, and she wanted to get Judy out of there. I don't remember my mother saying that Judy should leave; I don't think Mom did. I think it was a soap opera thing; that would be Judy's impression that Mom said that."

Judy's book *reads* like a soap opera. In fact, it has a *Mommy Dearest* hue to it, such as her bleak memory of her room in the mansion on Sunset Boulevard. She described it as a porch with walls of cold yellow brick. In truth, Judy and her nurse had the suite that Polly Ann and Sally shared prior to their marriages. Sally remembered Judy's early years as cheerful. She once told me that her daughter's nurse commented, "Why can't Gretchen be happy like Judy," to which Sally responded heatedly, "Because she's not Judy."

The book was so negative toward Loretta that I thought I understood why Judy needed to write about an interlude that Loretta denied ever happened: the warm and tender two hour visit between Judy and Gable. Without some positive interaction with her father, the reader might ask, "Wait a minute. Your mom is the one who raised you, took full financial responsibility for you. Your dad showed no interest, so why are you trashing her and letting him slide?"

The coverage of Judy's book sent Loretta to her bed time after time. In my own mind I referred to these spells as "Judy eruptions." I remember Loretta calling me in the midst of one, asking me to come see her in Palm Springs. When I arrived she was in bed with laryngitis, her usual reserve supplanted by one somatic symptom after another. I was in her room visiting, having a hard time hearing her because her voice was so faint, when Jean Louis entered the room. He lay down on Loretta's bed next to her and took her hand. Immediately I saw calmness come over her. I left the room. It was insightful to me. All along I had seen Loretta and Jean's marriage as all about Loretta caring for Jean. Now I witnessed reciprocation.

The saga of Judy's book took a bizarre turn when Judy contacted Loretta through an intermediary. Judy had spent the advance money from the publisher with anticipation of more to come after publication. The book hadn't been a big seller and now Judy owed $10,000 in taxes. Loretta, who had continued to help pay Judy's mortgage, was now asked to pay taxes on the income from a book that had trashed her. She quietly did so.

In November, 1994, seven months after Judy's book came out, Loretta sent the following message:

Dear Judy, I have decided that there can be no peace until I can forgive and be forgiven. So, if you feel the same way, I'd like to see you on the 23rd. I'll be in town at the house at 2:00. But, if you come, you must come in peace. No recriminations, no who did what to whom. If you don't feel this way, take your time because it will come to you. Love, Mom."

Judy quickly responded in the affirmative and the two met. Loretta was initially flustered but Judy was able to direct the conversation to safe territory and they visited for two hours. Afterwards, Both Sally and Peter cried on the phone when they learned of the meeting; prayers had been answered. Loretta expressed hope that the healing had begun but added, "It wasn't like CHRISTMAS EVE where we fell into each other's arms. That was a movie; this is real life and the hurt has run too deeply for both of us."

Chapter Twelve: Flying in Loretta's Palm Springs Orbit

Judy's book did not make any best seller lists, but at least it was published. By this time, I was four years into my project. Initially I thought that the first publisher who saw the book would grab it. That didn't happen. It was the beginning of a frustrating period during which The William Morris Agency sent it to one publisher at a time; a reply would not be forthcoming for at least two months, and then the answer would be no. That cycle would be repeated, time after exasperating time.

I had inherited some money after my mom died, but that wouldn't last forever. I had two other revenue streams. One was to go to my sister Carolyn's in Westfield, New Jersey, or my brother Kevin's in Connecticut, and paint their houses. Carolyn lived in a three story home in which I steamed off wall paper, repaired walls and painted. Kevin and Laura added a 2300 square foot addition that required both interior and exterior painting.

The other avenue was to return to my hometown of Kentland. The family business I had known growing up had been sold to British Petroleum, and my cousin Dick and his wife Elaina had created their own seed company, Frontiersman Seeds, which they operated with great success. I helped them with marketing, both planning and execution.

The fact that I was watching my money carefully made it easier to move in with Mark, with Loretta understanding exactly what the relationship was without having to acknowledge it. Mark was already living with Jim, a friend from his college days, and they invited me to join them in Laguna Niguel. I had been at my beach apartment for fourteen years, many of them lonely. However, it was a good place, I think a necessary place, to finally accept my homosexuality with dignity.

Simple things held Mark and me together. We could put a smile on each other's face and we shared a preference for a quiet lifestyle, not needing events to fill our lives. Simply put, we just liked being with each other.

Mark and Loretta met once. He found someone to repair a decorative bronze egret she wanted to place near the front entrance of her Palm Springs home. She was polite but cool toward him. I understood what was going on. She didn't like what he represented in my life. I don't think Mark really cared as he had little interest in Loretta's world. I was comfortable in both.

I had a nice office space in my new surroundings where I continued to work on the book. One complaint about my manuscript was its length. By this time, even I could see that my fascination with Loretta, everyone in her family, and all that happened in their lives had created a crowded canvas. I rewrote the book with broader strokes, this time without sharing the effort with Loretta. She knew that our endeavor was struggling and didn't try to interfere with re-writing this time around. Of course, the big remaining problem was addressing the Clark/Judy story. I had more to say now, but it failed to satisfy.

First, it wasn't in Loretta's voice; the details came from Polly Ann and Sally. Second, what I did have to say wasn't the story publishers wanted. I was no longer so naïve to believe that publishers would eagerly take what I had to give. They wanted to be in on a project from the very beginning and lay out the story they felt would be most marketable. They wanted a more satisfying Loretta/Gable story.

Regardless of the discouraging lack of movement with the book, I always enjoyed spending time with Loretta, and when she was in town she'd call and ask if I'd be interested in having dinner. I was fine with eating at her home; we had long gotten beyond the fantasy that Loretta could cook, so I was the one who did those honors.

One time she had invited Altovise Davis and her mother. Altovise was the young widow of Sammy Davis, Jr. She had been a former chorus girl and was quite attractive. A major theme that evening was how they all loved beluga caviar. I thought to myself, "No one at this table grew up eating caviar, never mind a preference for caviar from the Caspian Sea." But, then I remembered that Mrs. Davis was fighting the government over tax problems and had been since her husband's death. The beluga caviar conversation was escapist fare recalling better days. I found it interesting that Loretta and Sammy Davis, Jr. had been close friends and that many of her old movies in her library had been gifts from Sammy.

Sometimes Loretta just wanted to get out of the house. Since she preferred Beverly Hills fare, she would give me her credit card before we entered the restaurant so that it looked like I was paying. One time, when we were headed to an Italian place, Loretta told me that it was a favorite of the Mafioso. As we were sitting at our table, I quietly made a derisive comment about a couple next to us, a man in his sixties and a young blonde honey. Loretta responded, "Don't be so quick to judge. You've been good-looking your whole life. That man never has, and this is his way of evening the score."

Sometimes, I'd drive into Los Angeles to have lunch with Josie Wayne and she'd share some of her stories. On one of these occasions she opined why she thought John Wayne had wanted to end their marriage: "This was after he made STAGECOACH and everyone was treating him like a big star. Then he'd come home to the real world of a wife and four young children, and he said to himself, 'Who needs this?'"

Another time Josie shared a further memory: "A few years after we divorced, Duke came to the house to pick up Michael (their oldest son). Duke was waiting at the bottom of the stairs, and as I looked down at him, I realized that I was no longer in love with him."

Josie also related a couple of phone conversations that she and John Wayne had later in his life: "One day he called and said, 'Josie, I have a favor to ask. Pilar (his third wife and mother of his three younger children) isn't much of a mother. So when you're having a get-together with our kids, can you invite them to be part of your family as well?" Josie replied, "Sure, Duke," and she did.

The last time they spoke, he asked, "Josie, why don't you ever call and ask me for anything?" She replied, "Duke, I don't need anything." He rejoined, "Well, if you ever do, just call."

I always enjoyed being with Josie. She was fun and upbeat, plus, she offered some interesting tidbits regarding Loretta. One day she was talking about how well Loretta wore clothes and quoted Jean Louis, "'Loretta has never let a dress down,'" meaning that a designer would always be proud of the way she moved in his/her creation. Another day, I told Josie about sitting in Loretta's Beverly Hills living room and watching her descend the stairs, via a reflection in the entrance hall mirrors. Unaware that I was watching, she looked so imperious that the cameras should have been rolling. Josie's reaction was, "Long ago, Gretchen and Loretta Young fused as one."

Upon later reflection, I agreed that "Loretta Young" had permeated much of the individual I had come to know, but I felt I knew both Gretchen and Loretta. As the years went on, more of Gretchen surfaced in a number of ways. She became more honest in the sense that one tells a truer tale when allowing themselves to be vulnerable. For instance, the year after Judy's birth, Loretta was filming UNGUARDED HOUR at MGM, Spencer Tracy's and Gable's home studio. Both men were filming SAN FRANCISCO on a nearby soundstage, and they came together to visit Loretta. Loretta's original version (after the rewrite) addressed it the following way: "I was delighted to see them, both of them. I thought, 'Well, at least they're here at the same time.' All three of us knew the score: Spencer and Clark had both been in love with me and still were to some extent - I had been in love with both of them - and still was to some extent - but the past was the past - and there was no future, as far as romance. But, for the moment, everyone's good feelings flowed and it was exciting and stimulating. The whole set joined in the fun and I was full of gratitude for their loving attention."

Years later, I asked her about the same occasion. This time around she said, "Spencer was at his charming best, but I couldn't look him in the eye. As far as Clark, he was like a little boy, giving no thought to my struggle of bringing Judy into the world and then figuring a way to keep her. He had already started his affair with Carole Lombard and that was all he could think about."

Also, when we discussed KEY TO THE CITY the first time around, a film in which Loretta co-starred with Gable in 1950, she never addressed why she agreed to work with him again. Years later I brought the topic up, and this time she said, "I knew that the rumors about Clark and me had continued swirling over the years and I thought, 'No one would think that I'd have the guts to do this if the rumors were true.'"

Another example of Loretta letting the wall down was reminiscent of when Irene Dunne scolded Loretta for not returning her phone call, and Loretta understanding this as a higher degree of intimacy. One day Loretta and I were sitting in her living room, killing time before we left to go someplace. She said something and I responded that that wasn't quite right and then proceeded to correct her. I don't remember what we were talking about, but I clearly remember her response, "You're probably right. You almost always are. But you're being very petty. We were just having a little conversation, nothing important, something to pass the time. Now, the whole mood has changed." I felt the sting of her words, and for a few moments, didn't say anything and neither did she. However, almost immediately I saw her point. Sometimes, just being right isn't really very important.

Over the years I said things Loretta probably didn't appreciate. An example: when we went out for an evening, she usually didn't wear eye-liner. But there were times when she did, and I thought it made her look older. I certainly didn't say I thought it made her look older, but one day I told her that I thought she looked better without it. She patiently explained she only wore eye-liner when we were going someplace where she might be photographed, and that she photographed better with the eye-liner.

Some of what I learned from Loretta over the years was of a more profound nature. One day we were standing in her Beverly Hills kitchen, and I made a comment that I thought that most people would come to the conclusion at some time in their life that money really didn't bring happiness. My point was that after hugging to that hypothesis year after year, they'd see that it hadn't worked. Loretta responded, "I don't agree. Unfortunately, people just continue to think, 'If only I had *more* money, then I'd be happy,' but they never get to the point where they think they have enough. One has to be a person like me who has made millions, who has had beauty and fame, to realize that what the world has to offer isn't enough, that you have to turn to God for the answers."

Loretta's money, fame, and beauty did not always make her easy to be around. Greg Fischer told me once, "You've come into her life at the right time. Enough years have passed since the heady period of her television fame. The boss could be hard to take back then."

I also came to better understand the larger than life persona that Loretta displayed when she was in public. Sally told her she thought that Loretta was a big phony when she spoke in a different tone of voice to her fans. Initially, I tended to agree with Sally. But eventually I changed my mind. I remember being with Loretta in the lobby of a hotel in Providence, Rhode Island, where she was to receive an honorary degree from Providence College. I observed the now familiar manner in which Loretta responded to her fans. I realized that not only was she protecting herself with a role-playing shield but that she was playing the role people wanted. They wanted her to be larger than life.

Rejections on the book continued to mount, and months turned into years. My frustration was that The William Morris Agency wasn't marketing it in the most advantageous way. It was my opinion that Loretta had a huge, untapped reservoir of fans including Catholic women over the age of fifty who had grown up watching her television show and being told by their mothers that Loretta was a Catholic icon. This concept didn't appeal to the agency. Finally, I went to Loretta and asked her if it was okay if I contacted Norman Brokaw and request that I be allowed to find a publisher myself. Her eyes went wide at the suggestion but she agreed. Norman was gracious, if not warm, and told me that if I did find a publisher, he'd negotiate the contract. Having gone this far with my idea, I then rewrote the book yet again, with emphasis on anecdotes of Loretta living her spiritual convictions. I retitled the book, *Loretta Young: Journey of a Hollywood Soul*. This less-than-brilliant idea only led to more rejection, this time, coming directly to me.

Loretta continued to include me in her orbit and now much of that was in Palm Springs. She had people in for cocktails at least three times a week before hosting a dinner at her house or going out. She loved having fun and having fun people around. Greg Fischer told me that Loretta's mother had been much the same: work hard but then have fun. In the years I knew Loretta, I must have attended a hundred of these gatherings. They wouldn't be large, two or three couples, but the criteria was you had to be fun as well. Leave your troubles at home. Loretta had a theory. She said everyone has problems. The ones who seemed problem-free were just the better actors.

Loretta was queen bee at these little dinner parties and she enjoyed the role. But one day, she asked me if I thought she was too monopolizing. I truthfully told her no because she had such great stories. Nevertheless, she asked me to tug on my ear if I thought someone was unhappy about not getting their share of attention.

I only tugged my ear once. That was an evening when Jane Wyman was a guest. I had picked her up at her Rancho Mirage home and got off on the wrong foot. She was discussing something about her former television show, FALCON CREST and I had to admit I hadn't followed it. During dinner, Loretta was at her mesmerizing best. Miss Wyman was not amused. A tug of the ear and Loretta slowed down.

After I took Miss Wyman home and returned to Loretta's, I mused about trying to pitch myself as a biographer for Miss Wyman. I thought publishers would be interested in her years when she was married to Ronald Reagan. Loretta was pragmatic and wouldn't have minded if I found another subject. After all, the work on our book was done and she knew I needed the money. However, she cautioned me, "Don't do it. Jane's mean."

Loretta had close friends who were neighbors of Alice Faye, the former 20th Century Fox musical star. Her glory years coincided with the years Loretta spent at the studio. I remember sitting in the kitchen of Alice's neighbors with Alice sitting beside me. She was married to former bandleader and radio star Phil Harris who, by this time, was in his nineties. The subject of insomnia came up and Alice shared their solution. "When Phil and I can't sleep, we make a pitcher of martinis and that puts us right out."

I had heard from other sources that Alice wasn't a fan of Loretta's, so I wasn't too surprised at a particular incident. I was with Loretta's party as we entered a restaurant. Loretta was at the lead and out of earshot when I heard Alice, sitting in a corner as we passed, say, "Goodie, goodie. There goes Loretta Young!"

Loretta was on better footing with Bob Hope's wife, Delores. Sometimes I'd accompany Loretta to daily Mass when I was in Palm Springs. Quite often Delores would also be attending (along with her phalanx of body guards), and she and Loretta would visit after leaving church. Every time Loretta would introduce me and every time Mrs. Hope showed no indication of us having met before.

One day we were at the Beverly Hills home and looking at a picture in which Delores Hope was included. Pointing to the loose skin under Delores neck, Loretta said, "Really, there's no excuse for that. It's such an easy thing to take care of." That's as close as Loretta ever came to admitting to me that she had cosmetic surgery. That, and another comment, when she said, "The trick is to have just a little bit done at a time." I assumed that meant one would avoid that overstretched look I had observed a multitude of times traveling in her circle.

Whatever Loretta had done to maintain her face, it did not go unnoticed. One night we were out to dinner with a party that included Ronald Neame who directed such films as THE POSEIDON ADVENTURE, THE PRIME OF MISS JEAN BRODIE, HOPSCOTCH, and scores of others. Prior to being a director, he had been a cameraman, filming some of David Lean's early classics such as BRIEF ENCOUNTER and BLYTHE SPIRIT. That night someone asked him, "What is the most ideal face to film?" He directed everyone's attention to Loretta and said, "That's it. That's a perfect example. Oval shaped, large eyes, full lips, high cheekbones and a small nose. You can shoot from any angle." I could tell Loretta, in her mid-eighties by this time, was well pleased.

Also, about this time I remember a particular thought running through my mind regarding Loretta, Polly Ann, and Sally. Unlike my parents who slowed down from their mid-sixties on, these woman were doing the same kinds of things they did fifty years earlier, dressing up and going out or having each other over for cocktails. They seemed like they'd go on forever. Even Polly Ann, who was a heavy smoker.

One day Loretta drove Polly Ann to her doctor's appointment. Both women were hearing-impaired, and the young doctor was aware of this. So after asking Polly Ann if she was still smoking and she said yes, he walked behind the two women and mumbled, "Then why don't you just go ahead and goddamn kill yourself!" Polly Ann and Loretta both heard him and couldn't wait until they got out of his office so that they could double over in laughter.

Chapter Thirteen: More Rich and Famous

Loretta was staying at Polly Ann's and called me on a Sunday afternoon, inviting me to meet her grandson Evan. He was Peter's son by his first marriage and lived in Northern California. His wife and toddler daughter accompanied him; the baby was a beautiful little girl with blonde hair and blue eyes. The young family didn't stay long, but I was invited to remain for dinner. Later that evening, I asked Loretta, "Did that mean anything? Meeting your great granddaughter?" She hesitated for a second and then replied, "No, not really." It was the kind of honesty that helped define our relationship as the years had gone on. I think I would have been surprised had she said anything different. I had observed Loretta's relationship with her grandchildren. She was never a grandmother who counted the days until she could be with them. I don't think the investment was ever there.

Even with her children there was a distance. She had insightfully said that when they were growing up, she had meant to be a good mother but her career came first. And, as adults, I concluded that a different dynamic interfered with those relationships. One day I told her about my parents' 50th wedding anniversary and how my brothers, sisters and I arranged for a big celebration. We even erected a tent in the backyard for a guarantee against weather problems. Loretta's response was, "I can't imagine my children doing anything like that for me." I replied, "You have too much power in their lives, and I think they resent you for it." I then discussed the ways I thought she held power. I don't think she liked my assessment, but she didn't disagree.

My own family, and the one time with Mark, were the only people I introduced to Loretta. I knew she wanted it that way; so many people had tried grabbing a part of her over the years. Still, I'd have to say that Loretta was an extrovert; she was energized by social situations, and, of course, she loved being the center of attention.

I have a couple of Loretta's old address/phone books full of the Who's Who in Hollywood from the '40s into the '60s: the stars, directors and producers, as well as old and new Los Angeles money. When Loretta talked about these people, she'd invariably say, "Oh, I'm crazy about them," which I think she was but in the same way that high-powered couples from the business world float in and out of each other's lives with an intimacy that is both immediate and passing.

She had friends all over the country, even all over the world. One day I noticed a book titled *Holding the Stirrup* by Baroness Elizabeth Von Guttenberg on a book shelf. I asked Loretta if I could read it; I remembered my mother reading it when I was a kid and was curious. It was an account of the radical changes that took place in an aristocratic Germany family from the turn of the last century through the horror of the Third Reich. I read it in one night, and the next day I was riding with Loretta in the car and was telling her how much I enjoyed the book. She replied, "Let's call her when we get home." Sure enough, she was able to reach the Baroness in Munich, who had to be in her late nineties by then, and I had a chance to tell her how much I enjoyed her book and ask about her family.

However, as the years went by, I better understood why some of Loretta's friendships were so superficial and why she wanted them that way. I knew a couple of woman friends who would have been surprised that she thought of them as "fans" even after knowing Loretta for a couple decades and socializing with her often on a weekly basis. I was around long enough and close enough to see it from Loretta's viewpoint. These women were in her life because she was Loretta Young. They got what they wanted, and Loretta, in turn, benefited from the myriad tasks they assumed for her.

There was a married couple who often hosted Loretta to an evening out to the best restaurants in Beverly Hills, and I was often included. The wife headed a big charity ball annually and was able to solicit stars to draw in guests willing to buy a table, and invite their friends, with the expectation of mixing with the famous. For the rest of the year, our hostess liked to drop the names of these celebrities as if she was having coffee with them daily. Loretta invested very little into this friendship. They had her at their table and that's what they wanted. Loretta loved dressing up and going to nice places and that's what she got in return.

That same couple hosted a gala birthday party for Loretta at Jimmy's in Beverly Hills. I think they thought it was her eightieth but it was only her seventy-ninth. Nevertheless, they had rented a large room and it was decorated like winter-wonderland. I was told by another guest that the party cost twenty-five-thousand dollars.

While I was dancing with Loretta that evening, she asked me, "What are you doing?" I said, "I'm leading." She replied, "I can't remember the last time I danced with a man who led. Most of the time, they more or less stand still and I dance around them." I remember James and Gloria Stewart, both looking cadaver-thin and not much more animated while conversing, and thinking they should be home in bed. In fact, many of the guests looked like they should be home in bed. I didn't think that anyone was getting twenty-five-thousand dollars' worth of a good time.

There was another dinner party Loretta and I attended at a private home in Beverly Hills. I don't remember how Loretta was snarled into this one; she didn't know the host or hostess. The house was cavernous with long narrow windows in the living room. It looked like something out of a cartoon castle because the drapes ate up much of the wall space. Shortly after we arrived, Loretta and I were standing in the living room and wondering what her decorator mother, Gladys Belzer, would have thought. Just then, the hostess, apparently having observed us glancing about, approached. She must have assumed that we were favorably impressed, because she said, "I decorated this room myself. If you like the drapes, I can give you the name of my drapery maker in Paris."

I joined her another evening for dinner with a couple. Loretta had known the wife for decades and after she was widowed, married a guy who was some kind of low level Mafioso. Loretta's only stated objection about him was that he was an idiot.

There was an important hotel man who had hosted Loretta and me in New York and then also entertained us for cocktails and dinner when he was staying at the Bel Aire Hotel. Actresses Hope Lange and Elaine Stritch were also in the party. I could see that Loretta enjoyed the evening. I did, too. When we were driving back to her house from the Bel Aire Hotel, Loretta talked about our host and lamented that he was such a lost soul. "He doesn't have a clue what matters because, in his mind, it's all about *this* world."

I understood her point of view but was fascinated by how she could compartmentalize her various lives. There was her "cocktail friendships" life, and there was her "daily mass and say the rosary" life. There was her personal strong judgment about homosexuality, and there was her frequent evenings enjoying the company of gay men and lesbian women.

It's been written a number of times that Loretta, Rosalind Russell, and Irene Dunne were the three big Catholic female movies stars and that they were all close friends. It's true that they and their husbands socialized frequently but as Loretta once told me, "We never discussed any personal problems. We were all supposed to be movie stars leading perfect lives."

Loretta was also a genius at keeping the press at arm's length. Not long ago, on YouTube, I watched a 1986 interview with Loretta for ENTERTAINMENT THIS WEEK. She was promoting her television movie, CHRISTMAS EVE. I had to ask myself, "Who is this woman?" Loretta's interview struck me as a performance. Underneath the formality was a subtext that communicated, "Ask me the wrong question, this interview is over." I was glad that this wasn't the Loretta I knew.

Even within her family of origin, she had kept some distance. Sally told me that in the late '30s, Loretta was embroidering something with the letter "B." It was only later that her sisters discovered that she was engaged to a guy named Bill Buckner. Loretta freely admitted that she grew up in a world of her own dreams, with Mama being her base of reality. And, as mentioned earlier, Loretta never discussed Judy's origins with Tom Lewis during the sixteen years they lived as husband and wife. Just as weird: he never asked. Compartmentalization to the extreme!

As the years passed, I drew the following conclusions. The closest person in Loretta's life had been her mother. I also suspected that the same was true of Polly Ann and Sally in spite of their long-lasting marriages. By the time I knew the older sisters, I think their closest relationships were with each other, more so than with their children (but this is only my impression). One time, Loretta's son Christopher said to me, "I don't think that there's any love lost between those women." I didn't challenge him, but I didn't agree. Granted, he had grown up in the family and had a vantage point I'd never have. But I think that in the later years, I really had spent more time with them than he. My take was that, even though there were often cross currents that could spark old or present animosities, they turned to each other for bedrock support, the kind you get from those with whom you have shared your entire lives. I saw that as love.

I also know that Loretta had had a special love for her television crew, comprised mostly of men. Those eight years ebbed both high and low for Loretta. It was her own assessment that she was enjoying her career peak while, at the same time, her family life fell into shambles. Tom had moved to New York and, shortly thereafter, arranged for his sons to come visit. He then made a unilateral decision to keep them. The love of her crew was crucial sustenance for their vulnerable star and her feelings toward them ran deep. So much so that, after a year off, she returned to television in 1963 with the short-lived, THE NEW LORETTA YOUNG SHOW just to be working with them again.

Loretta received a letter thirty years later, indicating how her love for her crew had been reciprocated. Johnny London, Loretta's television producer sent her a note. She was so touched that she forwarded his letter to me with an accompanying note.

August 2, 1994
Ed, dear,
Johnny London – is one of the most unemotional men I've ever met in my life. He produced the L.Y. Show for 6 years – I think – Tom fired him – I rehired him. This is more than he <u>ever, ever</u> said to me in the whole time we worked together. It's worth quoting in the book. X L.

July, 1994 (written on yellow note paper)

Dear Loretta, Forgive the informality of this stationary but it's not an important letter. It may, however, remind us of happy times.

I was reminded that two years before I met you, I was the studio manager where Fred Zinnermann directed the classic "High Noon" with Gary Cooper and Grace Kelly. I negotiated the bank loan for "High Noon" and I was responsible for the final completion (in the days of "blacklist" politics with our writer, Carl Foreman being a problem). But all ok.
Last week, the Director's Guild of America declared Fred Zinnermann the <u>top director</u> of the last 50 years!

For me, "High Noon" and "The L.Y. Show" sort of overlapped in terms of time. After "High Noon" I worked at CBS for a while, then, suddenly I was working for you. I recall you (on stage) coming through that door. I was transfixed as I saw this unbelievably elegant lady simply coming toward the camera, perfectly costumed and confidently winning over her (vast TV) audience. I could not believe such a simple opening would overwhelm her millions of TV fans on NBC and over the world. Even the crew was caught up by your opening every week. In the years to come, many of your audience looked at our show to see the <u>entrance</u> rather than the filmed show which followed.

That would have pleased Fred Zinnermann, who always exploited dramatic simplicity such as the final scene with Gary Cooper and Grace leaving their small town all alone (Grace Kelly got $4500.00 for the <u>whole show</u>! Her first leading lady role.)

And Loretta, you had more great scenes during your career, than any other actress. So, dear Loretta, pause and reflect how good life has been to you. Love, Johnny London

Loretta could be very good to others. Her son Chris, his wife Linda, and myself were beneficiaries when Loretta agreed to be a featured celebrity on a two week cruise on Norwegian Cruise Line that took us from Fort Lauderdale, Florida, through the Panama Canal, and terminated at the Port of Los Angeles. This was so unlike her, allowing her celebrity to be used for commercial purposes. She did it for us. We could all go gratis as part of her entourage. Of course Loretta had the big suite while Jean and I shared a smaller cabin. I did serve a purpose. Jean would go walking on the deck and then forget the location of our cabin. After a half hour I'd go find him. I also got a huge ego boost in that every morning, there would be a Trivial Pursuit contest and various tables would vie for my participation.

Demographically, Loretta was a good choice for Norwegian Cruise Lines. In fact, when I first came on board, there were so many passengers being pushed in wheel chairs by their nurses, I felt I was on a hospital ship. However, I don't think NCL was enthralled with Loretta's level of participation. I'd been on other cruises when the celebrities would walk the deck and engage in conversation with whomever approached. Loretta didn't. She limited herself to some special appearances at which she shared some well-worn remarks. One of the best outcomes from that cruise was that Chris, Linda, and I forged a new kind of relationship, one just between us and no longer under the influence of Loretta's heavy shadow.

Back in Palm Springs, Loretta and Jean maintained a social presence, and I was part of Loretta's party for a couple of big events held at the Palm Springs Convention Center. One was a Tribute to Frank Sinatra which was a fundraiser for the Martin Anthony Sinatra Medical Education Center, named for his father and located next to the Palm Springs Desert Hospital. I was seated at a table directly across from Loretta when Bob and Delores Hope arrived at our table. Even before they had sat down, Frank Sinatra, who looked fine but shuffled like an old man, came from the next table to greet the Hopes. After he left, Bob Hope asked his wife, "Who was that?" She replied, "Sinatra." A little bit later, Loretta, who was seated between Bob Hope and Jean Louis, caught my eye and discreetly pointed fingers in both directions and rolled her eyes. She told me later that she was totally bored because Bob Hope was practically blind and deaf, and her own hearing impairment made it impossible for her to hear Jean's soft French accented voice over the din of a public venue.

The other event was the Palm Springs Film Festival of which Jean Louis was an honoree for Career Achievement in Costume Design. There was a VIP room to host the honorees and their families prior to the event. Tony Curtis was the biggest name on the roster. He was standing a few feet away as Loretta was engaged in conversation with Donald O'Conner, the host for the evening. Loretta referred to O'Conner as, "Little Donald O'Conner" (that was my first awareness that he had been a child/adolescent star,) and I observed Tony Curtis. He was wearing evening attire but no tie and his feet were shod with what looked like green alligator boots. What really caught my attention was his body language. He was leaning into a wall as if he wanted to disappear. He reminded me of the character he played in THE BOSTON STRANGLER, who was fraught with insecurity.

Producer Ross Hunter presented Jean's award. Jean had dressed Lana Turner in Hunter's IMITATION OF LIFE as well as his PORTRAIT IN BLACK. He also dressed Susan Hayward in Hunter's BACKSTREET.

Esther Williams accepted an award for George Sidney, a director for whom she had worked at MGM. Her remarks were rather lengthy, even though she was accepting the award for someone else. I wasn't surprised. Jean and Loretta attended a dinner party the night before at which Esther was seated next to Loretta. Loretta told me later that Esther talked non-stop. At one point, she leaned over to Loretta and asked, "Loretta, do you have money?" Loretta, somewhat startled by such a personal question, replied, "Yes, Dear, I do." Esther then explained the soundness of her financial situation from her swimwear and pool businesses. I had been surprised how people inquired about personal finances after my initial arrival in Southern California. Apparently Loretta and I shared this sensibility.

On the evening of the festival, Loretta wore a white chiffon gown with a red print. She asked Jean Louis to design a red velvet cape with fur trim. It would be Jean's last design.

While the awards were being presented, a woman with shoulder length blonde hair slumped in a wheelchair, was rolled near our table so that she could better hear the presentations. It was Ginger Rogers. I couldn't help but feel that the old guard of Hollywood might be hanging on a bit too long. Much would change and change quickly.

Chapter Fourteen: The Psychic Maid

Polly Ann died in January, 1997. Even though she was eighty-eight years-old and had been battling emphysema for years, her passing was a huge loss for her sisters. For Loretta and Georgiana, she embodied many of their mother's positive characteristics: non-flappable, pragmatic, resourceful. It was even a greater loss for Sally. Polly Ann had been her life-long best friend. One day Sally told me, "All my life, whatever problem I'd encounter, I always knew that Polly Ann was only a phone call away."

This would just be the beginning of coming losses. On her maid's day off (in Palm Springs) Loretta was attempting to rustle up something for brunch. Through the kitchen's sliding glass door, she could see Jean sitting in a lounge chair out in the garden. It was his favorite place to be. From there he could look beyond the crescent shaped pool, over the wall of deep pink bougainvillea, beyond to the massive San Jacinto Mountains. Jean would study all the colors in the mountains, ever-changing with the time of day. It was not unusual for Jean to drift into a nap, and not unusual for Loretta to come and gently wake him when she feared he was getting too much sun.

As she approached, there was something unusual about the position of Jean's body, as if he had tried standing and couldn't. She touched his shoulder to wake him and when he opened his eyes to look at her, something wasn't right. Loretta thought he was having a little stroke (he had had them before) and she said,

"Jean, I'm going to go call 911 and I'll bring back some ice packs." When she brought the ice packs and placed them around Jean's neck, his head turned slightly in response. Then Loretta realized she wasn't wearing her hearing aids and that she would need to go open the gate for the paramedics. Almost immediately, a squadron of paramedics whisked by her, rushing to Jean. Loretta was asked to wait in the kitchen, and within a few minutes a paramedic came to her. Loretta asked, "My husband's had a stroke, right?" The young man paused for a second, taking a deep breath, and said, "Oh, no, Mrs. Louis. Your husband has passed on." Loretta stood up and shrieked, "No! No! That can't be!" The paramedic held her very gently while she cried.

At the time of Jean and Loretta's third wedding anniversary, Loretta confided to Sally that she had never been happier than since her marriage to Jean. After Jean died, her family and close friends were somewhat taken back by the depth of Loretta's grief. It wasn't that they questioned Loretta's love for Jean, it was just that no one had seen Loretta so vulnerable.

Loretta decided to sell her Beverly Hills home. After the meaningful life she had lived in recent years taking care of Jean, she had little interest in jumping back onto the senior "A list" party circuit.

I was helping her pack the house during the first week of July, 1997, the week which Jimmy Stewart and Robert Mitchum died a day apart. Because both were huge stars, *The Los Angeles Times* continued running articles all week. I said to Loretta toward the end of the week, "I'm finding the articles about Robert Mitchum much more interesting." She replied, "I'm not surprised. Bob lived a much wilder lifestyle." There was some reproach in her tone, and I felt compelled to say, "I don't have any doubt that, with all the good he did in his life, that he's already in heaven." She then asked, this time with a hint of incredulity, "Do you really think so?" I said, "Oh, yeah, I really do."

This recalled another conversation that I had with her years earlier. I was quoting Jesus's commandment to "Love one another as I have loved you." Loretta's reaction was, "This love business is only for saints like St. Theresa of Lisieux. The rest of us have to work for our salvation." Again, I was reminded that Loretta was stuck in Pre-Vatican II Catholicism. In that vein, the challenge of life was represented by one big list that had to be checked off on a daily basis in the hopes of "earning" your salvation. On the other hand, whether Loretta realized it or not, she was a loving neighbor. A very literal example was a woman she knew through her church. She suffered chronic back pain and her husband had left her. Loretta paid the rent on her Beverly Hills apartment, feeling that the woman was suffering enough without the indignity of lowering her standard of living. Also, since I had that conversation with Loretta, she had nursed Jane Sharpe during her last months, not to mention, changing her whole life to become Jean's caregiver.

Another similar conversation: we were in the car one evening, and I made the point that God was a merciful God. He wasn't looking so much at our sins as He was so willing to forgive. This time, she was more receptive and said, "If you're right, I could have been having a lot more fun." I thought that was the end of the conversation, but a few minutes later, she added, "With my personality, I'm the kind who falls in love so easily, I probably would have been taken advantage of time and time again. I've probably been better off with the constraints."

It was on another car ride that I asked her, "What has been the biggest benefit of fame?" Without any hesitation, she replied, "Being able to meet other famous people. In my day, I met almost everyone." I asked, "John F. Kennedy?" "Well, I didn't exactly meet him, but one day I was getting off an elevator at the Royal Hawaiian Hotel in Honolulu as he was about to get on. Our eyes locked. He was a big flirt." I knew about all the times she had been to the White House so I skipped the other presidents. Instead, I asked, "Albert Einstein?" She replied, "Yes, I was his dinner partner one night. He was also a huge flirt." "Henry Kissinger?" "I sat next to him at a dinner as well; very charming, I can see why he was such a successful diplomat."

A few months after Jean died, Loretta found a buyer for her Beverly Hills home. This meant that I didn't see her as often but when I did, I stayed in Palm Springs a few days. Loretta had three very bountiful grapefruit trees in her back yard, and her pragmatic side hated to see any of the fruit go to waste. I'd climb the trees and pick them, leaving as many behind as she could distribute to friends and take the rest of them back to Laguna Niguel and hand them out to my friends. We had had a similar arrangement with Gallo Brute Champagne. Her friend, Maria Gallo, used to send it to her by the case. Loretta's reaction, "Oh, I can't serve this to my friends!" She gave it to me to give to my friends.

In the summer of 1997, A&E cable television network announced that they were going to do a segment on Loretta for their "Biography" series. I was asked to participate as were Chris and Judy. I initially thought that Loretta would see this as a hostile situation since the Clark Gable story couldn't be avoided, but, surprisingly, Loretta gave me the go-ahead to participate. It was an interesting experience. I was first interviewed by the producer and an assistant, both younger than myself. We sat at an outdoor café along Sunset Strip and chatted for a couple of hours. They said they'd be happy to have me and asked if I'd be okay without having questions in advance, that it would come across much more spontaneous if it were done in that way. It was fine with me.

The interview actually took place in a hotel suite. First, I went to makeup (administered in the bathroom) which was a strange experience. The guy wanted to draw eyebrows on me, saying that my eyebrows were so light that no one would see them. I replied, "They're so light, no one ever has and I'd look weird to my family and friends if all of a sudden I had eyebrows. Forget it." He did. The interview on camera lasted a couple of hours. The tricky part was that even though they continuously asked questions, I was never to respond as if I were answering a question. I was always to sound declarative as if I'm initiating the topic. For instance, if they asked, "What was the happiest time in Loretta's life?" I'd say something like, "Loretta was happiest in her professional life during her television years. This is when she felt she did her best work and had the most influence over her work. She was happiest in her private life twenty years earlier when she was the object of pursuit of so many men. She was and continues to be an incurable romantic."

Interestingly, if they asked Judy any questions regarding Clark Gable being her father, and this was after her book came out, they didn't use any of that material. Same with Chris. It seemed that they saved this dicey topic for me. The day we were filming, a production assistant was trying to help me shape my comments regarding Loretta/Clark/Judy into a more romantic mode. I responded that what she wanted wasn't really what happened. She replied, "I think it's important for Judy's sake. Every child deserves to think that they were conceived in love." I thought to myself, "Where does the truth come into this?" Just like with the book publishers, truth seemingly could take a backseat to the story they wanted. I felt like I navigated myself through by being honest yet discreet. Apparently not discreet enough for Loretta. I learned this from Chris's wife, Linda, but Loretta never personally took me to task.

Loretta had two successive maids while living in Palm Springs. The first one looked the part, and, as Loretta stated, "She served beautifully." This meant that when Loretta rang her little bell, this maid's comportment in serving a dinner party was movie perfect. However, she wasn't much of a housekeeper and Loretta eventually suspected that she was "toting," meaning that when she shopped for groceries, she included items that would go to her home but stay on Loretta's bill.

The second maid was Rosa, a San Salvadorian immigrant almost half as wide as she was tall. She didn't serve beautifully; it wasn't high on her list of priorities. But she was a wonderful cook, an excellent housekeeper, and most of all, she loved Jean Louis. Loretta swallowed hard, accepted Rosa's rebellious attitude and focused on how Rosa cared for Jean.

One day while visiting in Palm Springs, Loretta said to me, "Ed, I have to tell you something really strange. Rosa told me about her dream last night. She was standing on one side of a river, and on the other side stood Tom (Loretta's former husband and father of her sons) wearing a white suit. They had a conversation in which Tom told her things so personal it would be impossible for her to know any other way. I don't know what to make of it."

Was Rosa psychic? It sure sounded like she had some supernormal abilities. I had continued sending the book out to publishers and by this time I lost count of the rejections. I needed some reassurance that, eventually, all my efforts would pay. So, later that day, I asked Rosa, "What do you see in my future?" The look on her face conveyed that my question was bothersome and for a moment, I didn't think she intended to answer. Then she replied, "I see you working in the service of children."

I thought, "What! I have no interest working in the service of children. I'm a writer!" I dismissed Rosa's reading of my future as a misfire.

It may have been on that same visit that Loretta asked me to help her with a project. She had individual, professionally-shot photographs of her children that she wanted hung in the hallway leading to the bedroom suites. No guesswork allowed. Everything had to be measured to perfection. I had never seen these pictures before and asked why she decided to hang them now after having lived in the Palm Springs house for several years. She said that she wanted Judy to visit, and she felt Judy would be pleased. The 1985 reconciliation between Loretta and Judy had proved incomplete. There was no further acrimony, but as Loretta observed at the time, the hurt had run deeply for both of them. I was glad that Loretta was gearing up for another attempt.

On another occasion, after Jean Louis had died, Loretta asked me to clean out some file drawers with Jean's belongings because she had new use for those drawers. By "clean out", Loretta meant, "throw out"; I asked her if I could keep anything I found interesting and she said, "Sure."

There were a couple hundred of his sketches, mostly from his days when he had his own label and sold women's clothes through department stores. There were also a number of photographs as well as French magazines that carried stories and photos about Jean. The most interesting thing I found was a synopsis for a book Jean's wife Maggie had written. The intended book would be in Maggie's voice but tell the life-story of Jean Louis.

Chapter Fifteen: Loretta's Surprise Gift

Maggie Louis's book's synopsis failed to find an interested publisher, a status increasingly familiar to me. I was open for a change in my life and, from the beginning of my relationship with Mark, I was aware that he never intended to settle in California. Eventually he wanted to be closer to his family. I felt the same way in that I never considered California home. I often had the sense that I was swimming upstream in trying to navigate the pop culture. I was also at a point of near-desperation. The book was stalled and I was financially strapped. I was seriously looking at the Lotto as my salvation. So when Mark asked me if I'd consider moving to Houston, I was ready. Mark had been in contact with his former employer and found they were interested in re-hiring him. We traveled to Houston and I met and liked Mark's friends. Houston has a subtropical climate, and although humid much of the time, the lush greenery was authentic. It was unlike desert parts of California that were irrigated to look like Hawaii. I wouldn't be giving up on the book; publishers could be pursued from any origin. As for Loretta, she seemed to understand that it was time for me to move on.

A few weeks before the move, I was at my desk in Laguna Niguel when the phone rang. It was a very strange phone call from Sally. She had just been diagnosed with brain cancer, but she said, "I don't want to call Gretch or Georgiana and bother them." I tried to assure her that they'd want to know, but she demurred and then asked, "Will you call them?" I knew that Loretta was traveling and might be difficult to reach, but said that I'd call Georgiana right away. I asked Sally if she wanted me to come see her, but she declined.

I called Georgiana and related the message. Her reaction was, "Good God! Isn't this just like Sally, playing this for all the drama she can." I thought her reaction harsh but also understood that Ricardo was recovering from surgery, and now Sally would need her attention. Georgiana wasn't one who would back away from obligations. Another big one had just dropped in her lap.

When two people have conversations over a decade, lots of strange stories emerge. At different times, Loretta recalled occasions in which people had communicated misrepresentations about her. One time she was at a filling station, pumping her own gas, when a woman approached, saying, "I just want you to know how you touched the lives of people like me who have colostomies. Knowing that you do, too, and with such dignity, is an inspiration." That was the first time Loretta heard of such a rumor and felt bad that she had to disillusion the poor woman.

Loretta also told me that she was aware of rumors that she was a lesbian. Apparently, a Givenchy model, sitting next to her in a Paris restaurant, had heard the same. Loretta had to discreetly remove the woman's hand as it was slipping up her thigh.

The third story occurred when Loretta was walking to early morning mass while staying at the Louis apartment in Paris. She was wearing a mink coat and high boots, and a man stopped his car and propositioned her, thinking she was a high-priced call girl.

I made one final trip to Palm Springs to say goodbye. I don't remember much about that day but as I was leaving, Loretta said, "Come through the garage. There are two more cases of Brute Champagne you need to take with you." We stood in the garage for a moment, saying the kind of I-love-you's, that one would say under such a circumstance. I felt a bit let down, thinking that the emotions should be deeper. After almost ten years, it seemed anti-climactic.

Then Loretta said, "This heat (it was August) is deadly. Get in your car and turn on the air." I said, "Loretta, I don't have air-conditioning." She exclaimed, "No air-conditioning! No one should be driving in this heat without air-conditioning!" I responded, "You were driving in Palm Springs sixty years ago and no one had air-conditioning. You survived." With that, I kissed her goodbye, picked up the last case of champagne and headed to my car.

The next day I was packing for the move when Loretta called. She said, "I can't get it out of my mind that you don't have air-conditioning. When is the next time you plan to buy a car?" I said, "Probably within the year." She asked, "Will it be new or used?" I said, "Definitely used." Then she asked how much I was planning on spending. I said, "Maybe twenty-five hundred or three thousand." She said, "I'm sending you a check for four thousand so that you get something nicer, and I'm putting the check in the mail today, so that you'll have it before you move." I told her that wasn't necessary. She said, "I can't bear the thought of you driving without air. I'm sending the check." I thanked her. The truth was that the car I had was junk and probably wouldn't have made it to Houston. This way I could sell if for the few dollars it was worth, and Mark and I could drive the trip together.

We weren't in Houston a month when Sally died at age eighty-seven. She had deteriorated quickly. The year 1997 was devastating for Loretta. Within twelve months, she had lost her sisters Polly Ann and Sally, her brother Jack, and her husband Jean. Talking by phone with Loretta from Houston, Loretta admitted that, without realizing it, as long as Polly Ann and Sally were going strong, their longevity was like a shield protecting her. Now that shield had been removed.

I stayed in touch with Loretta by phone. Neither of us were big phone conversationalists, but I was surprised by and appreciative of how often she called. In one conversation, she told me that she and Judy rode to the cemetery together at Sally's funeral and that prompted an invitation to Judy to come to Palm Springs. The stated reason was that Loretta had clothes she wanted to give Judy. The ruse didn't surprise me; Loretta would never open the door to, "Come down Judy, and we'll talk everything out." Judy did come, and apparently, the visit went well. However, several months later, I mentioned how grateful she must be that her three children were back in her life. Her reply, "It's okay in small doses." I didn't ask for elaboration but it struck me as sad.

Chapter Sixteen: A Movie Star's Farewell

August, 2000, I was in Kentland working with Dick and Elaina for a few weeks. I got word from Linda, Loretta's daughter-in-law, that Loretta was slipping fast. For the past six months I had been aware that she had been diagnosed with ovarian cancer. I would visit with Loretta on the phone, but it was my calls to Linda in which the details of her illness were discussed. One day Linda called, telling me that Loretta was in the hospital and that it would only be a matter of days. Linda said, "Don't stop loving Mom. So few people ever have." I knew what she meant. Even though I thought that the sisters had a strong bond of love between them, it was often laced with undercurrents of conflict. Same with her children. For me, my relationship with Loretta was as if, somewhere along the line, we made an over-arching decision to ignore the flaws we saw in each other and only see the good. I sat down right away and wrote a letter to Loretta, hoping that it would arrive in time.

The following Sunday morning, I stopped at the grocery in Kentland before going to mass. As I was walking in, a woman I had known all my life, said, "Edward, did you hear Loretta Young died? It was on the radio this morning." Even though I knew it was coming, the news cascaded over me like lead. I was devastated but went on to church. The song played right before Communion was, "Taste and See." That had been her out-of-the-blue suggestion for the title of our book when we had begun working together. It didn't make sense then, but now I felt it was some kind of communication from Loretta.

Dick and Elaina were out of town that day so I spent it by myself, avoiding the newspapers and television news. I was just too raw. I did make arrangements to fly to Palm Springs for the funeral and arrived the day before. The wake was private but I was invited. I had a rental car but had a hard time finding the funeral home. As I was driving desert back-roads between Palm Springs and Cathedral City, there was tumble-weed blowing. It made me think about the first day Loretta, her mother and sisters arrived in Los Angeles. Loretta was age four and Polly Ann remembered that the street car went only so far because the paved road only went so far. Beyond were dirt roads carved through what had recently been orange groves. Loretta's professional image had been one of sophistication, but the flying tumble-weed reminded me that she was really of pioneer stock with the toughness to survive.

Less than two years before, *Vanity Fair* featured a current portrait of Loretta in their Hollywood issue. Her hair was now gray, and green drop-earrings brought out the green of her eyes. The caption read: "The Face," followed by copy exclaiming her enduring beauty. That night at the funeral home, viewing Loretta, I saw that the rigors of her illness had finally allowed the years to catch up.

The next day, as I was leaving the church, I spotted Josie Wayne with her daughter Linda. I approached her to say hello and she replied, "Ed, I can no longer see, but I recognize your voice." She went on to tell me that her daughter Toni was dying of cancer. In fact, Loretta had been in the room next to Toni's in the hospital.

Before her death, Loretta stipulated that her funeral be open to the public as well as the luncheon that followed at the Rancho Mirage Country Club. For a star often ambivalent about attention from fans, at the end, Loretta was generous. At that luncheon, I had a visit with Loretta's son Chris in which he told me that my letter did arrive and that he had read it to his mother just hours before she died. At this point, she had left the hospital, choosing to die at her sister Georgiana's home. She was in a semi-coma, but Chris told me that as he read my letter, a smile crossed her face and he could feel a slight tightening of her hand that he was holding.

Interment was a private affair. Loretta had requested that she be cremated, with her ashes placed in a sealed container. That container was then buried in her mother's grave site. I couldn't miss the symbolism. After a lifelong attachment to Gladys, Loretta was, once again, returning to her mother's embrace.

From my way of thinking, Loretta and I had one of those unconventional love stories, based on a friendship that grew through the years. I think she appreciated my forthrightness. One evening at a cocktail party in her Palm Springs home, someone asked me what I thought about something. Loretta interjected, "Let me warn you, if you ask him what he thinks, he'll tell you." Loretta wasn't used to people telling her things she might not want to hear, and I think she appreciated the honesty of our relationship (my lack of courage to openly tell her I was gay being a notable exception).

One of the last questions I asked her before leaving California: "Judging from where you are right now, have you had a happy life?" She replied, "Oh, yes. I think so. Certainly more so than unhappy." That summation did my heart good.

I think Loretta understood how much I loved her, how much I enjoyed being with her. I can't honestly say I forgot that she was Loretta Young, but I became very close to the woman underneath. She paid me the ultimate compliment of letting me in. One of the things I wrote in that last letter was that our book really wasn't as important to me as had been the opportunity to know and love her. I meant it. I still mean it.

How did it happen that Loretta and I had such a relationship? How did I get a ticket that night at the Los Angeles Museum of Art Bing Theater, when the event was sold out? Why couldn't she discard my letter that had sat on her desk for five months? Knowing so few people in Los Angeles, how was it possible that one of them would be Loretta's agent's good friend? I can't answer these questions, but I like to think that it was all meant to be, that things do happen for a reason.

I also realize to a greater degree how special an opportunity I had in knowing Loretta. Sometimes, I research her old movies on IMDb (International Movie Database) and read viewer's comments, people from all over the world hypothesizing what she must have been like. I really knew. They also rhapsodize about her beauty, and I better understand why Loretta thought it best that her fans never saw her age. They want her to always be beautiful.

Other times, I'll watch one of her films or an episode from her television show. There are certain scenes when she steps out of character and the Loretta I knew shows through; it's like a visit from an old friend.

I have lots of things around my home to remind me of Loretta. Apparently, when she was moving from the Beverly Hills house, and asked if I wanted this or that, I must have always said yes. I have stools from her kitchen, her gigantic wooden salad bowl, cocktail glasses and silver wine goblets, a silver candelabra, books, and lots of little kitchen gadgets(not that Loretta ever used them herself), religious artifacts, and the Christmas tree ornaments I observed the first day I met her.

I've seen enough of Loretta's films, many of them often, to offer the following, personal, observations: Her best silent film and the role that jump-started her career: LAUGH CLOWN LAUGH (1928). Her finest acting: MAN'S CASTLE (1933). Her most entertaining film: THE FARMER'S DAUGHTER (1947) for which she won an Academy Award. Her best soap opera movies: AND NOW TOMORROW (1944) and PAULA (1952). Her best comedy: BEDTIME STORY (1941). For insomniacs, the movies most likely to put them to sleep: THE TRUTH ABOUT YOUTH (1930) LADIES COURAGEOUS (1944). Her best Pre-Codes: EMPLOYEE'S ENTRANCE (1933) and MIDNIGHT MARY (1933). Most glamorous: THREE BLIND MICE (1938), CAFÉ METROPOLE

(1937), AND SECOND HONEYMOON(1937). Technicolor: KENTUCKY (1938). Photographed by arguably the silver screen's most revered cinematographer, Gregg Toland, in: PLAY GIRL(1932) and again, in THE BISHOP'S WIFE(1947). Closest she came to a film noir: THE STRANGER (1946). She did two westerns, THE LADY FROM CHEYENNE (1941) and ALONG CAME JONES (1945) but I prefer RACHEL AND THE STRANGER (1948) in which she played an Ohio pioneer woman.

Loretta did tell me before I departed for Houston that I was free to write any and everything I knew about the Judy/Clark Gable saga once she was no longer living. This meant that I was at liberty to include what she had told me personally.

It would take me years to return to the book. That's because my own life went on a roller coaster. In the same month Loretta died, Mark ended our relationship. Once again I had a meltdown, but this time, my recovery lead me back to school and I became a Registered Nurse. For fourteen years I worked on a psychiatric unit for children and adolescents. As it turned out, Rosa was right; I would work in the service of children.

Acknowledgment: for *Loretta and Me*

I thank Loretta Young for allowing me into her life. That entrée also opened doors to her family and friends and I thank them for their accessibility. I also thank Edward Russo, Dan Guio, Theresa Schoen, Malcolm Woodworth and Carolyn Benner, who edited this book at various stages of its development. I thank Salvador Iglesias for his generous access to Loretta photos and I thank Loretta's family for permission to use those photos.

About the Author

Edward J. Funk had been a ghost writer for business moguls who wanted to write their life stories to help promote their enterprises. The opportunity to work with Miss Young was quite different. It escorted him inside the golden age of film and the early days of television, both eras that had long held his fascination. His relationship with Miss Young has produced a trilogy of books about her; this is the second. Mr. Funk now lives in Indianapolis, Indiana.

Photo by Paul Robinson
Cover photo: permission to use from the Loretta Young estate
Cover design by The National Group

www.ingramcontent.com/pod-product-compliance
Lightning Source LLC
LaVergne TN
LVHW011912080426
835508LV00007BA/495